√ P9-CQG-425

WHAT IS IT CALLED WHEN . . .

. . . St. Nick is sued? A Claus action suit.

. . . decisions are handed down in June, July, and August? Summery judgment.

. . . actress Shepherd is hauled before a judge? A Cybill suit.

. . . Gloria Steinem takes the stand? A Ms. demeanor.

. . . someone testifies on behalf of the mayor of Palm Springs? Pro Bono.

. . . G. Gordon hires a lawyer? Liddygation.

. . . Ms. Brinkley is brought into a Texas court? Habeas Corpus Cristie.

RIB TICKLERS!
by Jeff Rovin

☐ **1001 GREAT SPORTS JOKES.** From football and basketball to bodybuilding, boxing, the rodeo, tennis, golf and every other sport—here are the funniest jokes ever to touch base and score in the great game of laughter! (169654—$4.99)

☐ **1,001 GREAT JOKES.** Over 1,000 jokes, one-liners, riddles, quips and puns—for every audience and every occasion. Among the topics skewered in this collection are: bathrooms, yuppies, hillbillies, sex, small towns, weddings, writers and much more! (168291—$4.95)

☐ **1,001 MORE GREAT JOKES.** Once again we've set a new standard in the wittiest, wackiest, most outrageous in adult humor. Here are jokes for every occasion—from raising chuckles from friends and family, to rousing roars of laughter from all kinds of audiences. Even better, the jokes are organized alphabetically by subject—so open up this book for a nonstop feast of fun from A to Z. (159799—$4.99)

☐ **1,001 GREAT ONE-LINERS.** The greatest one-line jokes, observations, and commentaries, for the first time, put together as a source of information and inspiration for anyone who wants to brighten up a conversation, a speech, or a piece of writing. Instantly prepare and swiftly serve up a feast of laughter. (164229—$3.99)

☐ **1,001 GREAT PET JOKES.** Laughter is raining down cats and dogs! (172612—$3.99)

Prices slightly higher in Canada

Buy them at your local bookstore or use this convenient coupon for ordering.

NEW AMERICAN LIBRARY
P.O. Box 999, Bergenfield, New Jersey 07621

Please send me the books I have checked above.
I am enclosing $_____ (please add $2.00 to cover postage and handling). Send check or money order (no cash or C.O.D.'s) or charge by Mastercard or VISA (with a $15.00 minimum). Prices and numbers are subject to change without notice.

Card #_____ Exp. Date _____
Signature_____
Name_____
Address_____
City _____ State _____ Zip Code _____

For faster service when ordering by credit card call **1-800-253-6476**

Allow a minimum of 4-6 weeks for delivery. This offer is subject to change without notice.

500 GREAT LAWYER JOKES

JEFF ROVIN

A SIGNET BOOK

SIGNET
Published by the Penguin Group
Penguin Books USA Inc., 375 Hudson Street,
New York, New York 10014, U.S.A.
Penguin Books Ltd, 27 Wrights Lane,
London W8 5TZ, England
Penguin Books Australia Ltd, Ringwood,
Victoria, Australia
Penguin Books Canada Ltd, 10 Alcorn Avenue,
Toronto, Ontario, Canada M4V 3B2
Penguin Books (N.Z.) Ltd, 182–190 Wairau Road,
Auckland 10, New Zealand

Penguin Books Ltd, Registered Offices:
Harmondsworth, Middlesex, England

First published by Signet, an imprint of New American
Library, a division of Penguin Books USA Inc.

First Printing, September, 1992
10 9 8 7 6 5 4 3 2 1

Copyright © Jeff Rovin, 1992
All rights reserved

 REGISTERED TRADEMARK—MARCA REGISTRADA

PRINTED IN THE UNITED STATES OF AMERICA

Without limiting the rights under copyright reserved above,
no part of this publication may be reproduced, stored in or
introduced into a retrieval system, or transmitted, in any
form, or by any means (electronic, mechanical, photocopying,
recording, or otherwise), without the prior written permission
of both the copyright owner and the above publisher of this
book.

BOOKS ARE AVAILABLE AT QUANTITY DISCOUNTS WHEN USED TO PRO-
MOTE PRODUCTS OR SERVICES. FOR INFORMATION PLEASE WRITE TO
PREMIUM MARKETING DIVISION, PENGUIN BOOKS USA INC., 375 HUD-
SON STREET, NEW YORK, NEW YORK 10014.

If you purchased this book without a cover you should be
aware that this book is stolen property. It was reported as
"unsold and destroyed" to the publisher and neither the author nor the publisher has received any payment for this
"stripped book."

ACKNOWLEDGMENTS

For their help in preparing this book, the author would like to thank Steve Burkow, Lou Petrich, Bob Dudnik, Judy Friedman, Joe Saffi, and other esq's—who, hopefully, will get a kick out of the finished product.

Thanks, also, to Matt Sartwell, Arnold Dolin, and Ed Stackler for editorial assistance.

INTRODUCTION

"The first thing we do," said the rebellious Dick in *Henry VI, Part 2*, "let's kill all the lawyers."

Maybe Shakespeare was just being cranky when he wrote that, or maybe a solicitor had made a mess of one of his contracts.

In any case, the sentiment he expressed in 1597 remains strong nearly five hundred years later. But since killing all lawyers is impractical (they've proliferated like dandelions since the days of the Bard), consider this book of lawyer, judge, courtroom, and jury jokes a compromise: voluntary mans-laughter.

Attorney Wengler was defending Ardolino for murder.

"Ladies and gentlemen of the jury," he said as he began his closing argument, "I'm going to prove beyond a doubt that my client is innocent. In exactly one minute, the supposed victim is going to walk in that door, fit and full of life!"

The courtroom fell silent, and for sixty seconds no one moved. A minute came and went, and when no one had arrived, the lawyer said, "Ladies and gentlemen—the alleged victim did not show up. But the very fact that you watched the door suggests an element of *reasonable doubt*. And if such a doubt exists, you cannot find my client guilty."

The trial ended, Ardolino was found guilty, and Wengler was both surprised and depressed. Walking over to a member of the jury, he asked, "How could you fail to acquit him? You yourself were watching the door . . . you had your doubts."

"That's true," said the juror. "But the

woman sitting next to me was watching Ardolino, and *he* wasn't watching the door."

Father Kahrs arrived at the attorney's home just as Dr. Iovino was leaving.

"And how is attorney Quirk doing?" the clergyman asked.

"I'm afraid our friend is lying at death's door."

Father Kahrs shook his head. "Poor Quirk. About to face his maker and *still* lying."

Q: What's an attorney's favorite drink?
A: A Subpoena Collada.

The attorney walked up to the owner of the restaurant and said, "my client is suing your establishment because he failed to find a single clam in the clam chowder."

"Then I can save you a trip back," the proprietor said. "Guess what he didn't find in the angel food cake, either?"

The electrician finished replacing a faulty switch in the attorney's home, and presented him with a bill.

"One hundred dollars for a half-hour's work?" the attorney cried. "That's ridiculous! Why, I'm a lawyer and *I* don't make that much."

The electrician replied, "When I was a lawyer, neither did I."

The devil appeared in the lawyer's office one night.

"How'd you like to make a little deal?" said the red-skinned demon. "For the rest of your natural life, you will defend only the richest people in the world, you will never lose a case, you will have any woman you want, and you will become the most revered lawyer of your generation.

"In exchange, when you die, I will claim your immortal soul, which will burn in the scalding pits of hell for all eternity."

Sitting back and stroking his chin, the lawyer said, "Okay. What's the catch?"

Kevin's new counsel came to the case with no knowledge whatsoever of his client or the charges. Visiting him in prison, he asked, "How long will you be in for?"

"A week."

"What did you do?"

"I killed my wife,"said Kevin.

The lawyer looked at him. "You killed your wife and you only get a week in prison?"

"That's right. After that, they execute me."

Q: What's the difference between someone being sued and two lawyers arguing in a jet?

A: One's a defendant, the other a plane tiff.

"You're the most incompetent lawyer a defendant ever had," sneered the condemned man.

"I did my best," the lawyer protested.

"Sure, but you objected when this one gave her testimony, and you objected when that one gave his testimony."

"What's wrong with that?"

"Buster," said the condemned man, "when the jury came in and found me guilty—*that's* when you should have objected!"

Attorney Smith and attorney Wesson met at their country club.

"I hear you're representing old man Eastwood's estate," said Smith. "How much did he leave?"

Wesson replied, "Why, everything, I imagine."

Q: Why can't lawyers go to the beach?
A: Stray cats keep throwing sand on them.

Murray faced the judge. "Your honor, I don't see how you can charge me with forgery. Why, I can't even write my own name!"

The judge said, "It's not your own name you've been charged with writing."

On the other hand, there was a lawyer who was so fond of arguing he wouldn't eat anything that agreed with him.

The lawyer paced before the witness in the stand.

"Would you tell the court at what time the murder occurred?"

The witness tapped her chin. "I think—"

"We aren't interested in what you think," said the attorney. "We only want the *facts*."

The witness frowned. "I'll give them to you, but I can't talk without thinking. I'm not a lawyer, you know!"

Then there was the attorney who represented a man arrested for selling marijuana. After losing in the supreme court, the attorney resolved to get the laws changed in a joint session of congress. . . .

Attorney Vin Papa said to eyewitness Elaine, "Are you sure my client was in the convenience store exactly three minutes?"

"Yes, sir."

Papa drew back his jacket sleeve. "When I say *begin*, I want you to tell me when exactly three minutes have passed." Papa glanced from the witness to his watch. "Begin."

Elaine stared blankly ahead, and exactly three minutes later she said, "Stop."

Papa was flabbergasted, and he lost the case. When it was over, he cornered Elaine in the hallway.

"I still think my client was innocent, but you've got to tell me: how did you know when three minutes were up?"

"Easy," she said. "I looked at the clock on the wall behind you."

After a controversial trial, the attorney wound up his lengthy closing argument by stating, "What I want from this trial is social reform. What I want is judicial reform. What I want is congressional reform."

From the back row of the jury someone shouted, "What I want is chloroform."

The lawyer said to his client, "Well, if you really want my honest opinion—"

"I don't," said the client. "I want your professional advice."

Q: What's the difference between a lawyer and pickets at a van line?
A: One moves to strike, the others strike to move.

The judge looked up at Wim and asked, "Have you ever been up before me?"

"I don't know," said Wim. "What time do you get up?"

⚖️

"You've been brought here for stealing," the judge said to the defendant.

"Great," said the man. "What are we taking, and from who?"

⚖️

A doctor, an architect, and a lawyer were lunching together and got to discussing whose profession was the oldest.

"The Bible says that Eve was created from Adam's rib," said the doctor. "Obviously, a surgeon was involved."

"Perhaps," said the architect, "but it's also written that the earth was created from chaos. Someone had to have designed the earth, which suggests that an architect was called upon."

"That may be," said the lawyer, "but who do you think created the chaos?"

Jody found Lisa sitting at the fast food establishment, drinking coffee.

"Lisa, how are you?"

"Terrible. My husband's been handling an important case and he's been at the office every day for two months, even on weekends, working all hours."

"That's too bad," said Jody, "but I thought you two didn't get along. Has absence made the heart grow fonder?"

"No," Lisa said. "The jury hands down its verdict today and he'll be coming home."

A sleazy-looking man was hanging around the bench, and the court clerk asked, "Are you the man accused of robbing the jewelry store?"

"No," said the man, "I'm the dude who did it."

"You've been arrested three times for the same crime," the judge said to Mr. Porter. "Aren't you in the least bit ashamed?"

"No, your honor," Mr. Porter replied. "I don't believe a man should be ashamed of his convictions."

The judge said to Dupre, "Before I pass sentence, have you anything to offer the court?"

"Your honor," said Dupre, "I would if I could, but the lawyer took my last dime."

The attorney asked the defendant, "Where were you on the night the murder occurred?"

"I was with a friend of mine."

"Another lying, shiftless, greedy soul?"

"Yes sir," said the defendant. "He's a lawyer."

Q: Where do lawyers hang their hats?
A: Legal pads.

The judge was aghast when he heard the verdict and asked the jury, "What *possible* reason could you have had for acquitting the defendant?"

"Insanity," said the foreman.

"Yes," said the judge, "but all of you?"

The lawyer phoned his rich client, Morgenthau.

"I've got bad news and terrible news," said the attorney. "The bad news is, your wife just paid ten thousand dollars for a picture that's going to be worth several million in a few weeks."

"That's *bad* news?" said Morgenthau. "I can't wait to hear the terrible news!"

The lawyer said, "It's of you and your secretary."

A judge and a priest were chatting about their respective powers.

"I believe mine are more extensive," said

the priest. "You can say to a man, 'You will be shot at dawn,' and that is of course frightening, but I can say to him, 'You will be damned for all eternity.'"

"True enough," said the judge. "But when I say to a man, 'You will be shot at dawn,' he most definitely *is*."

Q: What's guaranteed to make a plaintiff walk away from a lawsuit with a million bucks?
A: Start by asking for twice that.

The district attorney said to the alleged mobster, "Where were you between six and eight?"

The mobster thought for a moment, then replied, "In first grade."

The gunshop owner took the stand and the prosecutor asked, "Would you please tell the court the exchange which took place when Mrs. Farley walked into your store?"

"Yes, ma'am. She said, 'I'd like a gun for my husband.' I said, 'What kind would he like?' And she said, 'I don't think he cares. He doesn't even know I'm going to shoot him.'"

⚖

Then there was the attorney who was a tad concerned about his mobster-client's claim that he was innocent of having a rival beaten. Seems he sent a get-well card to the man—three days before it was needed.

⚖

The judge said to the defendant, "Aren't you embarrassed to be seen here so often?"

"Not at all," said the man. "This place seems very respectable to me."

⚖

The prosecutor sought a concise way to sum up the trial. Rising, she said, "Ladies and gentlemen of the jury—all I can say is that if Moses had known the defendant, there would have been two or three more Commandments."

The sailor took the stand.

"Would you please tell the court if you recognize either the defendant or the plaintiff," said the prosecuting attorney.

"Beg your pardon, sir," said the sailor, "but would you explain to me what those words mean?"

The lawyer's eyes narrowed. "Shame on you! How can you take the stand as a witness in a murder trial and not know those basic terms?"

"Sorry, sir."

The lawyer said, "I'll rephrase the question. Tell the court where you were when the accused is said to have struck the victim."

"Well, sir, I was abaft the binnacle."

"And would you please explain what those words mean?"

"Shame on you!" said the sailor. "How can you work on a case about murder on a boat and not know those basic terms?"

Millionaire Klaus von Belleau was accused of murder. He went to see Jake Blossom, a prominent attorney.

After listening to the attorney's thoughts and fee structure, von Belleau said, "I like your ideas, but your price is much too high. Why, the attorney I saw yesterday only wanted half that amount."

"Then by all means use him," said Blossom, "since you won't have to pay him at all."

"What do you mean?"

Blossom said, "Your heirs will."

"Where did the car hit Mr. Carson?" the attorney asked the doctor as the trial got underway.

"He was struck at the junction of the sternum and clavicle."

"Excuse me," interrupted one of the jurors, "but I've lived here all my life, an' there's no such place as either of those."

The attorney was explaining his courtroom style to the law students.

"When the facts are on my side, I hammer the facts. When the law is on my side, I hammer the law."

A student asked, "What do you do when neither of those is on your side?"

The lawyer replied, "I hammer the table."

Then there was the unlucky soul who was picked for jury duty and found guilty . . .

. . . the prosecutor who described herself as a talent scout—for Sing Sing . . .

. . . and the crook who paid his legal bill and complained, with some justification, that the wrong man was on trial.

The teacher was asking her first graders what their parents did for a living.

"My dad builds houses and my mom is a speech therapist," said little Shay.

"My dad is a chemist and my mom runs a catering service," said little Craig.

"My mom is a homemaker and my dad owns and operates several illegal houses of prostitution," said little Jenny.

The teacher was aghast and, during recess, she went to the office and called Jenny's mother.

"Your daughter told the class that her father owns a series of brothels. Why would she say such a thing?"

The woman replied, "The truth is, her dad's a lawyer—but you could never tell *that* to a six-year-old."

Q: What's the difference between a promiscuous lawyer and a studious lawyer?
A: One spends more time outside his briefs than in them.

Then there was the playful probate attorney who described his fee as heir fare . . .

. . . and the lion tamer who hired a lawyer to check the new claws in his contract.

The yokel went to see a lawyer. "I want my marriage cancelled," he said.

"You mean annulled?"

"That's right."

"On what grounds?" the lawyer asked.

The yokel said, "I just found out her pappy didn't have a license for the gun!"

Q: What do an Italian sports match and a powerful lawyer have in common?

A: One's a big-a tourney and so's the other.

The young attorney gave a rambling closing argument that lasted nearly an hour. When it was the opposing counsel's turn, he rose and scored double points with the restless jury by stating, "Following the example of my colleague, I give you the case without a closing argument."

The lawyer said to the locksmith, "What were you doing when the brothel was raided?"

The locksmith replied, "I was making a bolt for the door."

Then there was the judge who established the express court, for criminals with eight convictions or less . . .

. . . and the driver who hit a pedestrian, knocked him twelve feet in the air, and had to hire a lawyer. The cagey attorney sued the pedestrian for leaving the scene of an accident.

Fitzwilly was a distinguished-looking gentleman who seemed anything but the kind of man to go peering into a woman's window while she was undressing. But he was caught doing just that, and now he was on trial.

"What were you doing outside with binoculars so early in the morning," his attorney asked.

"I was birdwatching," said Fitzwilly. "That's my hobby, you see."

"Birdwatching. And you simply decided to switch from thrushes to Ms. Buxley?"

"Not at all," said the gentleman. "Oh, Ms. Buckley *is* very nice, but the black-breasted canary in her bedroom—now *there's* a specimen!"

Q: What do you call fifty lawyers at the bottom of the ocean?
A: A good start.

"I'm guilty," the defendant told his lawyer

in prison. "I robbed the store . . . but I'm *so* sorry I did it, I'll never do anything like that again."

"I believe you," said the lawyer, "but when you take the stand, we've got to maintain your innocence."

The defendant looked at him. "Y-you mean you want me to lie?"

"I mean," said the lawyer, "you can't be 'conscience stricken' until you're hatched."

The judge said to Benson, "The charge against you is throwing your mother-in-law from a fifth-floor window. How do you plead?"

"Guilty," said Benson. "I—I guess I wasn't thinking."

"I'll say," said the judge. "You could have seriously hurt an innocent passerby."

"I'm sorry," the judge said to the young man, "but for creating a public nuisance by romping around naked, I must commit you."

"For shame!" said the man. "You've no right to commit a nuisance!"

Senior partner Dysart summoned attorney Olsen to his office.

"I realize you brought in five million dollars of new business last year, but you've been rude to the other partners and abusive to your assistants, you've bribed judges, had rival attorneys beaten up, and I know about the affair you've been having with my daughter.

"I'm sorry to say this," said Dysart, "but one more lapse and you're dismissed."

Then there's the chronic divorcee who keeps getting richer by decrees . . .

. . . the divorce attorney who described himself as an expert in avoiding long division problems . . .

. . . and the lady attorney who never gets a speeding ticket. Whenever a policeman stops her, she simply lays the law down.

Q: How do we know that Moses was a law-giver and not a lawyer?
A: The Ten Commandments are short and concise.

Shelly asked Pauline, "How was your divorce attorney?"

"Let me put it to you this way," said Pauline. "Some lawyers are good; some are lousy. Mine was both."

The Pope arrived at the Pearly Gates and was shown to his apartment. As an angel helped him settle into his spartan room, the Pontiff saw a limousine drive by with a man inside. The nattily dressed fellow was drinking champagne and frolicking with lady angels. The car pulled up in front of a sprawling mansion and the man went inside.

"Who is *that*?" asked the Pope.

"That's attorney Peter Pollock."

"An *attorney*?" said the Pope. "Good lord! I was the head of the Catholic church and I've got this small room. What could he *possibly* have done to merit such luxury?"

"The truth is," said the angel, "we've got dozens of popes up here, but Pollock is the only lawyer we've had in centuries."

Speaking of Heaven, attorney Gantcher showed up at the Pearly Gates where he was interviewed by St. Peter. Beyond him, in a brilliant ball of light, sat God Himself.

"What good deeds have you done to entitle you to enter this place?" St. Peter asked.

"Well," said the lawyer, racking his brain, "I once gave a quarter to a homeless man."

"Is that all?"

"No," said the attorney. "I also gave fifty cents to a charity one Christmas."

"Is that it?"

"Well . . . yeah. I guess so."

Suddenly, a voice boomed from the ball of light. "St. Peter—give the man seventy-five cents and tell him to go to hell."

The attorney asked the plaintiff, "What happened when the defendant walked up to you?"

"He asked urgently, 'Have you seen a cop around'? And I said, 'No, I haven't.' "

"What happened then?"

The man replied, "The sonofabitch robbed me."

Then there was the lawyer who had considerable disdain for juries. As he put it, "It's disconcerting to realize that your fate is in the hands of a dozen people who weren't bright enough to get out of jury duty."

"I didn't rob the parking meter," the defendant told the prosecutor.

"But twenty-three people say they saw you walk up to the meter, hit it with a hammer, and leave with the coins!"

"They're wrong," said the defendant. "When I left the meter, there wasn't any change in it."

Then there was the law firm that fired a partner who was a bored member . . .

. . . and the dairy farmer who paid his legal fees in a quart of law . . .

. . . and the trial attorney who was so good his adversaries knew they'd end up with a loss-suit on their hands.

The ambulance rushed to the scene of the accident where a lawyer lay amid the wreckage.

"Stay calm," said the paramedic, working frantically. "You've had a serious crackup."

"Oh, my Jag . . ." he moaned. "My poor, poor car."

"Look," said the paramedic. "I wouldn't

worry about your car. Your left arm's been ripped off!"

The lawyer groaned, "Oh, my Rolex! My poor, poor Rollie!"

Q: What do you call a lawyer who doesn't chase ambulances?

A: Retired.

Enderby showed up at his lawyer's office. "I want a divorce."

"But you were just married last week!" the lawyer said.

"I know. But my wife said I'm a lousy lover."

"And *that's* why you want a divorce?"

"No," said Enderby. "Because she knows the difference."

Arthur went to see the divorce attorney.

"We're splitting because, after two years, my wife found out I've been using a sexual aide to make love to her."

"You mean you're impotent?" said the attorney.

"That's right. But we always made love in complete darkness, so she never suspected."

"I see. And now that she knows, she wants to leave you?"

"No," he said. "We're splitting because she's pregnant."

The judge said to the teenager, "I'll let you off with a hundred-dollar penalty *this* time, but next time it's prison."

"You mean I get the weather report," said the boy.

"The weather report?"

"Yes, your honor. Fine today, cooler tomorrow."

One bailiff said to another, "I feel like telling the judge to drop dead again."

"What do you mean *again*?"

"I felt like telling him that last week, too."

Then there was the woman who sued her doctor for malpractice. It ended up a wash: she got a free organ transplant, but she had to give her lawyer an arm and a leg.

The judge was sitting next to an inebriated man in a bar.

" 'Afore I leave," the man said to the bartender, "gimme a Halley's Comet." The man turned to the judge. "A Halley's Comet ish wine an' lime an' absinthe an' it'll send y' into space. Ever try one?"

"No," the judge said sternly, "but I've tried idiots who have."

Q: What's the difference between a carpet in an entranceway and a judge who charges an attorney with contempt?
A: One's a foyer liner, the other a lawyer finer.

The judge said to Rupert, "That'll be sixty dollars or sixty days."

Rupert thought for a moment and said, "I could use the sixty bucks, thanks."

The lawyer said to the defendant, "Why were you arrested?"

"I went to an Adam and Eve party."

"Which is—?"

"Leaves off around two A.M."

Q: What is alimony?
A: The screwing a man gets for the screwing he got.

Q: What is the motto of an honorable American attorney who handles a dead man's estate?"

A: "Hands off the fee in the home of the bereaved."

The prosecutor asked the gunman, "Why did you shoot the plaintiff? Couldn't you have hit him from behind and taken his money?"

"No," said the defendant, "I hadn't eaten in seven days."

"So?"

The man said, "That makes one weak."

Q: What's the difference between a lawyer trying a case and an explosion in a coal mine?

A: Nothing. Both are a lot of noise coming from a little opening.

An Hispanic youth was standing trial for robbing a WASP. The judge clearly favored the plaintiff, and it didn't take long for the defense counsel to become annoyed.

"Your honor," she said, "what would you do if I called you a dumb racist bastard?"

The judge huffed. "Why, I'd have you suspended for contempt of court."

"What if I only thought it?" she asked.

"In that case, there's nothing I could do. People are free to think what they wish."

"Then let the record show that I think you're a dumb racist bastard."

⚖

Then there was the jury that found the girl guilty for having killed her parents. However, the judge chose to be lenient because she was an orphan. . . .

⚖

The wealthy man told his son, "Manfred— I expect you to earn your money the same way I did, through hard work."

"But you inherited your fortune, dad," said the lad.

"True," said his father, "but it was damn hard work keeping it from the lawyers."

The district attorney said, "Mrs. Olsen—after you put the arsenic in the stew and served it to your husband, didn't you feel the least bit of remorse for what you were doing?"

"I did," she said softly.

"And when was that?"

Mrs. Olsen replied, "When he asked for seconds."

The midget rose when the judge called his name.

"Mr. Gustafson," said the judge, "you've been named in a paternity suit. Have you anything to say for yourself?"

"It wasn't my fault," said the little man. "A couple of friends put me up to it."

Q: What happened when Hilda, the octogenarian attorney, started rambling during a trial?

A: The opposing sides set Hilda out of court.

Then there were the lawyers who formed a new firm, Boyd, Dewey, Costa, Lott, and Howe . . .

. . . the other attorneys who formed Wein, Ever, Lye, Toody, Cort . . .

. . . the divorce lawyer who advertised, "Satisfaction guaranteed or your honey back . . ."

. . . and the lawyer whose client was injured in the crash of a police car and a cement truck. The incident turned him into a hardened criminal.

Q: What's the difference between the author of *Born Free* and a perjurer?
A: Nothing. They're both fond of lion.

The judge asked Hubert, "Would you explain to the court why you stole your neighbor's canary?"

"I took it for a lark."

The judge said, "I sentence you to sixty days and a visit to an optometrist."

"It's been a lovely two years, and I hate going through with the divorce," Maurice said to his attorney. "Did you know that I fell in love the second time I saw my wife?"

"Not the first time?" said the attorney.

"No. The first time, I didn't know she was rich."

Q: What do you get when you sleep with a judge?
A: An honorable discharge.

Then there was the motorist who hired an attorney after his car was towed. He claimed there was nothing wrong with leaving his automobile beside a sign that read, "Fine for parking. . . ."

Nelson took the stand and his attorney asked, "Why did you steal the apple from the fruit stand?"

"I wasn't feeling well," he said, "and I thought some fresh err might do me good."

Orville fell in love with Doris Woolworth, the woman he was representing in a divorce suit. Unable to get her out of his mind, he was asleep one night when he began to mutter, "I love you, Doris. I want to marry you just as soon as I can get a divorce."

Awaking and feeling his wife's furious eyes upon him, Orville shouted, "Objection, your honor! I request that Mrs. Woolworth's lover be removed from the court!"

Q: What do you call a lawyer who sells legal expertise to whores?
A: A prostituting attorney.

Then there was the argumentative law student who graduated cum loud . . .

. . . and the tenacious lawyer who couldn't prevent his client from being hanged. However, he did sue for whiplash.

"Look," the defendant told the judge, "I can prove I'm not guilty of the crime. If I could just have some time—"

"So ordered," said the judge. "Thirty days."

The man looked at the check he received after winning his suit against the city.

"Wait a minute!" he said to his lawyer. "This is only a third of the full amount!"

"That's right," said the attorney. "I took the rest."

"*You!*" screamed the man. "*I* was the one who was hurt!"

"You forget. I provided the intelligence required to build the case, the expertise to find precedents, and the oratory to convince the jury. Any asshole could fall down a manhole."

The lawyer said, "Ms. Rachlin, would you tell the court why you stole the plaintiff's car?"

"Sure," said Rachlin. "It was parked at the cemetery, so I figured what the hell? The owner won't be needin' it no more."

Speaking of cemeteries, the elderly couple was strolling through an old churchyard when they saw a headstone that read, "Here lies a lawyer and an honest man."

The woman said, "What do you know? Back then they were burying them two to a grave."

The woman called her attorney. "My husband was hit in the butt by a car, and I want you to represent him."

"Of course," said the lawyer, and began making notes. "You say he was hit in the backside?"

"Yes."

"Rectum?"

"Are you kidding?" the woman said. "The poor guy was flattened!"

Then there was the divorce attorney who sent out five hundred perfumed Valentines signed, "Guess who . . . ?"

. . . and the lawyer who refused to defend his sibling because he was too close to her case. As he explained it, "How can I be a brother and assist her at the same time?"

Another lawyer, Glenn Strange, stipulated in his will that he wanted his headstone to read, "Here lies an honest lawyer."

When his son asked why, the lawyer said, "So everyone will know who's buried there."

"How will they know that?"

The lawyer explained, "Because when they read it, they'll say, 'That's Strange!' "

The sailboat enthusiast was suing the shipping company.

His lawyer asked, "Would you tell the court what happened when the ship filled with string crashed into your sailboat?"

"Yes, sir," said the boatsman. "I was stranded."

In a twist to that case, the shipping company sued a lighthouse keeper, claiming the accident occurred because his beam was dim. Turns out he was cooking omelets at the time, enjoying eggs on his beacon. . . .

Irving went to see a divorce lawyer.

"Why are you here?" his attorney asked.

"Well, my wife and I haven't had much of a sex life for several years, so I asked what I could do to make her interested in sex again. And she told me."

"That sounds like a good, honest start," said the lawyer. "So why are you here?"

Irving said, "She told me to leave."

Q: What's the difference between an orthodontist and a lawyer?

A: You get your money's worth from the orthodontist's retainer.

Then there was the human cannonball who sued the circus because they refused to discharge him . . .

. . . the man who sued the mail carrier because he was tired of receiving partial post . . .

. . . and the lawyer who explained a contingency fee to his client. "If you lose, I get nothing. If you win, you get nothing."

There was also the prosecuting attorney who grilled the Mafia kingpin late into the night. Finally, the don broke.

Sadly, the woman decided to leave her sculptor husband because she never saw him: night and day, he stayed in the basement working on marble statues. Her lawyer was able to obtain the divorce by painting the man as a low-down chiseler. . . .

Q: What's the best way to lose one to two hundred pounds of fat?
A: Hire a divorce lawyer.

"Is there anything you'd like to say before I pass sentence?" the judge asked the convicted crook.

"There is, indeed," said the crook. "Would you please go out and have a nice, satisfying lunch on mc?"

Ubu was shopping in the cannibal market when she was stopped cold by the price of a particular item.

"Hearts, twenty dollars a *pound*!" she said to the owner. "M'tumba, you're selling livers for a dollar a pound and brains for a dollar-fifty. Where do you get off charging so much for heart?"

"These are from lawyers," said the owner. "Do you know how many we had to kill to get a pound of heart?"

"Actually," Mrs. Scott told the divorce lawyer, "my husband and I do have *one* thing in common—the inability to communicate."

Willie was hit with a paternity suit, and to prove his innocence his lawyer took a rather unusual tack.

While Willie was on the stand, his attorney told him to unzip his pants and take out his member. After Willie had done so, the lawyer walked over and grabbed it.

"Members of the jury, I ask you to take a good look at this miserable little thing—this shriveled, scrawny, immature organ." He shook it at the jury. "Does *this* unimposing strand look like it could *possibly* father a child?"

Willie said from the side of his mouth. "Hey, bub—if you don't let go, we're going to lose this case!"

Q: Why didn't the shark eat the lawyer?
A: Professional courtesy.

Mrs. Stillman went to see her lawyer. "I want a divorce because of illness."

"Who's sick?" the lawyer asked.

"I am," she said. "Of my husband."

Lemmon was accused of burning down his warehouse, and the trial dragged on for months. It ended with his acquittal, after which the insurance company paid him one million dollars.

A week later, he got the lawyer's bill and hit

the roof: it was for eight hundred thousand dollars.

Storming into the attorney's office, Lemmon said, "Where do you get off charging me so much?"

"I got you off, didn't I? You got two hundred grand, didn't you?"

"Sure," Lemmon said, "but for that kind of dough you'd think *you* started the fire!"

Marge walked into the divorce lawyer's office.

"My husband won the lottery and told me to pack for a trip," she said.

"That's wonderful!"

"No, it's *awful*," she said. "When I asked whether I should pack for warm weather or cold, he said he didn't care—as long as I was out by morning."

Q: What's the difference between romance and divorce?
A: One's a courtin' time, the other a time in court.

Mrs. Ketchum's divorce lawyer said to Mr. Ketchum, "Isn't it true you married my client because you knew her father left her a fortune?"

"No!" Mr. Ketchum protested. "I'd have married her regardless of *who* left her a fortune!"

"Before I can hear your case," the lawyer said to a prospective client, "I'll have to have a one-hundred-dollar retainer."

Since time was crucial, the client didn't argue and paid the money.

The lawyer said, "For that fee, you're entitled to ask me two questions."

"Why, that's fifty dollars a question! Isn't that rather high?"

"Not really," said the lawyer. "Now what's your second question?"

Then there was the attorney who represented a transvestite hooker accused of male fraud . . .

. . . the lawyer who believed in taking his case to the jury, one juror at a time . . .

. . . and the woman who broke a mirror and went to see her lawyer. He was able to get her four years of bad luck.

"Gee whiz," said the defendant, "this courtroom is hot as an oven!"

"What did you expect?" said her attorney. "This is where I make my bread."

The lawyer went to the whorehouse and, flashing one thousand dollars, asked for Becky Smart. He was shown to the attractive young hooker, and had a great time with her.

The next night, the lawyer returned and, once again putting one thousand dollars on the table, asked the madam for Becky Smart. Once again, he had a great time.

This went on every night for a week. On the seventh night, the lawyer was dressing and Becky said, "Listen, big guy—where you from?"

"White Plains," he said. "Woodlands Avenue."

"Really!" said the whore. "That's amazing! I just won a paternity suit with a guy who lives on Woodlands!"

"I know," said the lawyer. "He's my client—and here's the last of the seven grand he owes you."

The not-very-bright young man was brushed by a passing taxi, and an opportunistic lawyer convinced him to sue the cab company. Taking the stand, the man was questioned by the cab firm's attorney.

"Mr. Jenkins," said the lawyer, "you were hit on the shoulder and that has caused damage to your neck muscles, is that correct?"

"That's right, sir."

"Would you mind showing the court how far you can move your head?"

The man craned slowly and with apparent

pain to the left. His head went halfway down to his shoulder.

"I see," said the attorney. "And how far were you able to move it before the accident?"

The man bent his head all the way to the side.

Q: To what tribe do all lawyers belong?
A: The Sue Nation.

Mrs. Tipton said to her class, "A millionaire dies and leaves twenty million dollars. One son gets a third, a daughter gets a quarter, and a third son gets a fifth. The rest goes to his brother. What does each one get?"

Little Peggy answered, "A lawyer."

Q: How are lawyers like sperm?
A: Only one in three million does any real work.

Then there were the research scientists who decided to replace their lab rats with lawyers. They didn't become as attached to them.

Another research lab also began substituting lawyers for rats. After all, there's no shortage of lawyers.

A third lab elected to use lawyers because there are some things a rat just won't do.

Mrs. North telephoned the offices of Mudge, Posey in New York.

"I'm looking for a criminal lawyer," he said to the receptionist.

The receptionist replied, "Aren't they all?"

Then there was the lawyer who pointed out to his client that a divorce is no different than a tornado or an earthquake: no matter what you do, there's a good chance you'll lose your house. . . .

Q: How does a JAP get an LL.D.?
A: Marriage.

After delivering his closing remarks, Attorney Blyth took his seat beside an associate.

"Look at the jury, will you?" said Blyth. "Every one of them has tears in his eyes."

His colleague replied, "That's because they know your client is doomed."

Losing yet another case, attorney Blyth said to a colleague, "I've really got to think about going into another line of work." He snickered. "And to think—I wanted to be a lawyer badly."

"Hey," his colleague said, "at least you got your wish."

As one millionaire said to another, "Where there's a will, there's a lawyer. . . ."

. . . and as the other millionaire said, "Lawyers! You can't live without them, you can't die without them."

While donning his robes, the judges said to a colleague, "What would you give a sixty-two-year-old prostitute?"

"Oh," the colleague said, "about thirty bucks."

Q: How does a lawyer say, "Screw you?"
A: "Trust me."

The court-appointed attorney met with his client Herman in jail.

"I don't understand why you're here," said the lawyer. "All you did was rob your kid brother's bank."

"That's right."

"This is ridiculous. I'm going to call your brother and see if he'll drop the charges. Where does he work?"

Herman said, "The Washington Bank on Fifth and 45th."

Then there was the lawyer who sent a third bill to his client along with a note: Long time, no fee . . .

. . . and the attorney whose closing arguments made for a wordy cause.

⚖

Q: What's black and brown and looks terrific on a lawyer?
A: A Doberman.

⚖

"Another attempted robbery?" the judge yelled at Stevens. "Didn't I tell you I never wanted to see you in this courtroom again?"

"Yes sir. And that's what I told these officers, but they wouldn't listen!"

⚖

A lawyer is someone who . . .
   . . . writes a fifty-page document and calls it a brief.
   . . . buys a pair of shoes, making three heels.
   . . . approaches each new case with an open mouth.

. . . never tells a lie in court as long as the truth can do as much damage.

. . . understands that laws are society's guidelines, but helps criminals read between them.

. . . likes to have the last word, but never seems to get to it.

. . . works in wide, open spaces—surrounded by teeth.

. . . helps you get what's coming to him.

. . . never heard the adage, "Talk is cheap."

. . . would rather know the judge than the law.

. . . prevents someone else from getting your money.

Rival judges Charles and Gordon happened to show up at the same party and, during the course of the evening, both got drunk and were arrested for disorderly conduct.

Arriving early for their court hearings, they found the place deserted and decided to try themselves.

Charles heard Gordon's story, then said, "Disorderly conduct, eh? Since this is a first offense, I fine you fifty dollars."

Then Gordon took the bench and heard Charles's story. When he was finished, Gordon said, "This is the second such case we've heard in the past few minutes and I intend to put a stop to it. That'll be one thousand dollars and thirty days in jail."

One attorney said to another, "As soon as I realized it was a crooked deal, I got out of it."

The other attorney asked, "How much?"

Q: What's the difference between a lawyer and the dry cleaner?
A: A lawyer loses your suit *then* takes you to the cleaners. . . .

Then there was the exhibitionist who got himself arrested so he could be tried in public . . .

. . . the fickle jury that returned its verdict . . .

. . . and the old lawyer who didn't die, she just lost her appeal.

Jackson ran over to the car after witnessing the accident.

"How badly are you hurt?" she asked the driver of one car.

"I don't know," he said. "I'm a doctor, not a lawyer."

Q: What do you call a smiling, sober, courteous person at an ABA symposium?
A: The caterer.

After listening to the lawyer outline his strategy, the man asked, "Why is a divorce so damned expensive?"

The lawyer replied, "Because it's worth it."

Muybridge, the portrait photographer, walked out of church and saw O'Hara, the lawyer, drive by in a new BMW, a beautiful woman in the passenger's seat.

The photographer turned his face toward heaven. "I don't understand it, lord. O'Hara is an avaricious attorney, a philanderer, and a cheat who takes money from those who can't afford it. I come to church every morning and pray every night. Why should a lawyer have all the comforts of life, while I have so few?"

The clouds split, a face appeared in a sea of white light, and a voice resounded from above. "Because he doesn't *nag* me the way you do!"

Then there was the lawyer who opened a Japanese restaurant called So-Su-Mi . . .

. . . and the co-defendants in Prague whose lawyers requested individual trials. They said that, in such instances, they always asked for separate Czechs.

"Tell me," the reporter asked the attorney, "are lawyers honest?"

"Let me put it this way," said the attorney. "I borrowed forty thousand dollars from my father so I could go to law school, and I paid him back after my first case."

"That *is* admirable," said the woman. "What was the case?"

"He sued me for the money."

Q: What do you call a court of law with twelve black men?

A: A hung jury.

The prosecutor asked the witness, "How do you know that the car belonged to the Mafia?"

"Simple," said the man. "I checked the hood."

"The hood?"

"Yeah. He was in the trunk."

The defense attorney was questioning Mr. Feld.

"Now, sir--you claim to have seen the car accident clearly, despite the fact that it was late at night and you were three hundred yards away. Tell me—just how far *can* you see at night?"

"Oh . . . at least two hundred thousand miles."

"That's impossible."

"No it isn't. How far is the moon?"

One white-collar jailbird said to another, "I'm here for robbing from the rich and giving it to my lawyer."

Q: What's the difference between a defendant and a long-winded lawyer?

A: One is tried by the jury, the other tries the jury.

The uneducated defendant muttered something during the trial and, overhearing him, the judge had him gagged.

His lawyer, who had been addressing the jury and hadn't heard what was said, approached his client during a recess and removed the gag.

"What did you say that pissed him off?"

"Ah does not know," said the defendant. "I was prayin', an' all ah said was, 'God am de judge.'"

Judge Linus Pauley said, "Mr. Austin—I understand you wish to be called Colonel Austin. When did you serve in the military?"

"Actually," drawled Mr. Austin, "Colonel is jest a title of respect—like when they call you the Honorable Linus Pauley. It don't mean anything."

Old Mr. Able was writing out a new will.

"How many children have you?" his attorney asked.

The feisty Able replied, "That, I'm afraid, we will not know until I die and this will is contested."

The newspaper inadvertently printed an obituary of the elderly lawyer, and he threatened to sue unless they printed a retraction.

The next day, the following notice appeared:

"We regret that the report of the attorney Burk's death was in error."

Q: What's the difference between a rooster and a lawyer?

A: A rooster clucks defiance. . . .

Then there was the attorney who was fond of saying, "Where there's a will, there's a delay . . ."

. . . the other attorney who tried to get his kleptomaniac client off by saying that she simply had the gift of grab . . .

. . . and the Israeli attorney who began his opening statement, "Ladies and gentlemen of the Jewry. . . ."

When his secretary strolled into the office at ten minutes after ten, the congressman said, "Honey, we may be sleeping together, but who says that gives you the right to come in late for work?"

Smiling sweetly, she replied, "My attorney."

Then there was the personal injury lawyer who mistook feet for meters and found herself overruled . . .

. . . and the lawyer who got in trouble for making a motion to this miss. . . .

Q: What's the difference between a corpse and a lawyer in a courtroom?

A: One just lies there, the other just lies, there.

The attorney said to Jezebel, "I think you're a perfect juror for this case. Why do you want to be dismissed?"

"I don't want to be away from my job."

"You mean to say they can't get along without you for a few days?"

"Indeed they can," said Jezebel. "I don't want them to realize that."

Mr. Schneider stood up in court. "As God is my judge, I do *not* owe my ex-wife any money."

Glaring down at him, the judge replied, "He's not. I am. You do."

The lawyer was admitted to the condemned man's cell, and the prisoner ran up to him.

"What's the word on the governor's pardon?"

"He'll be released next week."

The lawyer asked the plaintiff's ex-employer, "You say you fired my client due to illness."

"That's right."

"But she never missed a day of work."

"That's also correct," admitted the employer. "I was just sick of her never doing any work. . . ."

Then there was the attorney who believed in the "mining" approach to law. She kept the gold and gave her clients the shaft. . . .

Attorney Watts asked attorney Ohm, "Was your client shocked over the death of his wife?"

"Shocked?" said Ohm. "He was electrocuted!"

Ohm was, however, able to get the doomed man a reduced charge . . .

The lawyer went to his client's electrocution, then stopped by to see the man's mother.

"Wh-what did he have for his last meal?" she asked.

The lawyer replied, "Juice . . . then toast."

The lawyer tried to make her feel better by noting that at least the woman's slothful son had had a job at the very end. He was a conductor.

Q: What's the difference between a lawyer questioning a witness and crosseyed bugs?

A: One is queries with answers, the other ants, sirs, with queer eyes.

Curious to find out if pets picked up any of the characteristics of their owners, Dr. Harryhausen borrowed cats that belonged to a basketball player, a psychiatrist, and a lawyer.

Putting the hoopster's cat in the room with

a bowl of food, Dr. Harryhausen watched through one-way glass as the animal ignored the food and swatted a ball around the room. Next, he let in the psychiatrist's cat. The animal just sat in a corner, observing the other cat.

Then he put in the lawyer's cat.

Without hesitation, the animal screwed the other two cats, ate all the food, then took a nap.

The attorney said to his client, "I can get you an acquittal, but it'll cost two hundred thousand dollars."

The client's mouth fell open. "Two hundred grand? All I did was clip a police cruiser!"

"I know," said the attorney. "But if you pay me that much, we can plead insanity and no one will dispute it."

The defendant was acquitted and phoned his wife with the good news.

"My lawyer got me off," he said. "Trouble is, now I'm gonna have to rob someone to *pay* her. . . ."

The judge looked down at O'Brien. "You're charged with public drunkenness. What's your plea?"

"Not guilty," said O'Brien. "Why, I'm as sober as you are, your honor."

"Thirty days. Next case."

Then there was the divorce attorney who was fond of describing alimony as bounty on the mutiny . . .

. . . the law professor who wrote a textbook that was bound to do well . . .

. . . the self-impressed attorney who was always me-deep in conversation. . . .

. . . and the super-dedicated law student who studied his books from A to Zzzzzzz.

The judge said to Mrs. Pica, "You're seeking a divorce. What are the grounds?"

"What's left after you make coffee."

"No, I mean what are your charges?"

"Sears, American Express, Visa—"

"Mrs. Pica, I'm asking *why* you want a divorce!"

"Oh," she said. "My husband and I don't communicate."

The poor, old widow was charged with stealing a shawl, and attorney Richardson took her case. He won an acquittal and, in a show of charity, agreed to charge her only one hundred dollars. The woman's bony hand reached into her purse and, shaking, she handed him a third fifty-dollar bill by mistake.

Realizing what she'd done, the attorney was faced with a profound moral dilemma: Should he tell his partners?

The alleged crook was not cooperating with the swearing-in.

"Hold up you right hand," said the judge.

"I can't, your honor. It got hurt when I was arrested."

"Then hold up your left hand."

"I can't," said the defendant. "That got hurt, too."

The judge raged, "I will not allow you to testify in my court unless you hold up *something*."

"Okay," said the defendant. "Let's have your wallet."

Q: What's the difference between a dead lawyer and a dead snake lying in the street?
A: There are skid marks in front of the snake.

It was the first time the young man had ever been in court, and the judge wanted to make sure he understood how things worked.

"You realize, don't you, what will happen if you don't tell the truth, the whole truth, and nothing but the truth?"

"Yes," said the man. "I'll probably go free."

Then there was the lawyer who got his client a suspended sentence. He was hanged.

Yet another lawyer pleaded with the judge to give his client a short sentence. The judge was happy to oblige:

"Life."

Q: Why does Los Angeles have the largest number of lawyers and New Jersey the largest number of landfill sites?

A: New Jersey got first pick.

After her attorney had reviewed the evidence in the murder case, Paula asked, "How should I plead?"

The attorney said, "On your knees."

The prospective juror said to the judge, "I can't possibly serve in this case. Why, just looking at that woman I'm convinced she's guilty!"

"Madam," said the judge, "that's the prosecutor."

The lawyer went to talk with his client in jail.

"Hello," said the prisoner. "I'm 24601."

"Please," said the lawyer, "I'd rather you not use your pen name."

Q: What's the difference between a probate lawyer and a Cockney hat?

A: One protects heirs, the other 'airs.

When the judge had passed sentence on O'Malley, the defendant said, "Your honor, you might as well add another three years to my sentence."

"Are you saying you've committed another crime?"

"Well," O'Malley answered, "in a minute or two, I'm going to beat the shit out of my asshole attorney!"

As he was dragged out of the courtroom, the killer shouted to his lawyer, "Twelve Americans out of a quarter of a billion say I'm guilty. You call that justice . . . ?"

Mr. Curtis said to the judge, "You have to grant me a divorce from my wife. For the ten years we've been married, she's smoked in bed."

"And you feel that's a reason to divorce her?"

Curtis replied, "I do, your honor. She smokes herring."

The judge said to the convicted thief, "Not only did you remove five thousand dollars in cash from the premises, you also took two peach pies and a pair of new shoes. Will you tell the court why?"

"Your honor," said the crook, "didn't anyone ever tell you that money alone does not bring happiness?"

On the opposite end of the social scale, young Danforth had been shut out of the will, and the attorney tried to console him.

"You know," said the lawyer, "money isn't everything."

"I know," said Danforth, "but it's the only thing I really need right now."

The celebrity divorce lawyers were talking.

"I just found out why Robin Givens didn't change her name when she married."

"Right," the other attorney said. "She didn't want to be known as Robin Tyson."

The prosecuting attorney said to the defendant, "Your first wife died from eating poisoned mushrooms, your second wife died from eating poisoned mushrooms, and now your third wife has died because the brakes failed and her car plunged off a cliff. How do you explain that?"

The defendant said, "She wouldn't eat the mushrooms."

Then there was the survey which reported that eighty percent of all lawyers were bottle-fed, which proves that even their mothers didn't trust them . . .

. . . and the survey which proved that it's not much tougher to buy a judge than it is to buy a gun.

There was also the post-office blunder: they issued a stamp honoring the legal profession, and discovered that people were spitting on the wrong side. . . .

"Ms. Ackerman," said the attorney, "you testified that your neighbor shot her husband—yet you didn't actually see it happen?"

"No, sir."

"When you ran over, did you see any powder marks on his body?"

"Yes, sir," said Ms. Ackerman. "That's why she shot him."

"You're accused of loitering by the bank and casing the place," the judge said to the man. "How do you plead?"

"Innocent, your honor."

"Then would you tell the court what you were doing there?"

"I was picketing."

"Picketing? The arresting officer says you were just standing there, looking in."

"I was waiting for a sponsor."

Mr. Mahrs, an advertising executive, went to see a lawyer about a client's long-overdue bill.

"You asked your client to pay the bill?" the lawyer asked.

"I did."

"And what did he say?"

"He said I should go to the devil, so I came right here."

The mobster said to the attorney, "If you get rid of this racketeering charge, I'll pay you one million dollars."

"You've got a deal," said the attorney. "Produce some witnesses."

The mobster did so and, sure enough, the lawyer got an acquittal.

"I'll take that million dollars now," the attorney said.

The mobster replied, "Produce some witnesses."

Humperdinck got screwed in a divorce settlement, and went for a nice, long drive. Finding himself in a small town in Texas, he stopped at a crowded bar, went in, and began drowning his sorrows in alcohol.

"Freakin' lawyer," he muttered after his third drink. "He's no damn good. *None* of them are any good, the horses' asses!"

Leaning over the counter, the bartender said, "I'd keep it down, if I were you."

"Why? One of these men here a lawyer?"

"No," said the bartender. "This is horse country."

"Lawyers, lawyers, and more lawyers!" the widow sighed to her friend. "I've gotten so sick of lawyers for the will, for the estate, and for the family, that sometimes I wish Harry hadn't died!"

Then there was the man who was convicted of battery and was placed in a dry cell . . .

. . . and the lawyer who worked well into the night to break the young widow's will.

The judge glowered at Mr. Harvey.

"After hearing how you behaved during the course of your marriage, I've decided to grant your wife a divorce. I'm also giving her two thousand dollars a month in alimony and child support."

"Thanks, your honor," said Mr. Harvey. "I'll try to pitch in a little something myself as well."

The woman went to see a divorce lawyer. "I want out of my marriage. My husband's sex drive is making me crazy."

"How do you mean?" asked the lawyer.

"He wants it infrequently."

"I see," said the lawyer. "Is that one word or two?"

Q: What's the difference between a porcupine and a pair of lawyers in a BMW?
A: The porcupine has its pricks on the outside.

Q: What's another difference?
A: The porcupine's pricks serve a purpose.

The attorney said to the woman in the witness box, "Would you please state your name."

"Eleanor."

"Full name, please," said the lawyer.

"Eleanor Roosevelt.'

The attorney looked at her. "You *are* aware that that's a rather familiar name."

"It should be," she said. "I've lived here for over a half a century!"

Bob and Anne remained friendly after their divorce. Six months later, Anne said, "Bob—I've been dating the judge who handled our divorce, and now he wants to marry me. What do you think?"

"I think," said Bob, "he wasn't listening to the evidence."

Q: What's the difference between a faithful lover and a convicted bank robber?
A: One's tried and true, the other tried and through.

Then there was the lady lawyer whose elderly client, Mr. Bromsgrove, attempted to molest her. She had him hauled into court and tried for assault with a dead weapon.

Turns out Mr. Bromsgrove had been in court before for the same offense. As the judge put it when passing sentence, she was sick of seeing him weak in, weak out. . . .

Fortunately, the case against Mr. Bromsgrove was settled in small-claims court.

Mr. Percy went before the judge.

"Do you have a lawyer, Mr. Percy?"

"No sir."

"Can you afford to hire one?"

"No sir."

"In that case," said the judge, "the court will appoint one for you."

"That won't be necessary, sir."

The judge folded her hands. "What, then, do you propose to do about the charges that have been brought against you?"

"Gee," Percy said. "I'll forget about 'em if you will."

The attorney said to the jury, "My client was arrested for running naked down the street, but I intend to show the court that he was *not* naked. He was simply wearing a one-button suit."

Lucien had a big family to support, and stole five thousand dollars from his bank. However, after a few days he began to feel guilty and confessed to an attorney.

"Do you think you can steal ten thousand more?" the lawyer asked.

"I—I suppose so," said Lucien.

"Do that, then come back to see me."

Lucien returned the following day with the money, and his attorney drafted a letter to the bank. It read, in part, "Your head teller, Lucien Welles, stole fifteen thousand dollars from your bank to help his family in a time of crisis. Through diligent effort, he has managed to scrape together ten thousand of that, which he will gladly repay if you agree not to prosecute him. . . ."

Attorneys Jackson and Pollock were told to approach the bench, where Jackson was given a severe dressing-down for his hostility toward a witness. However, before the judge was quite finished, Jackson turned and stalked back toward his client.

"Counsel," said the judge, "are you trying

to show your disgust with the court by turn-
ing your back?"

"No, your honor," said Jackson. "I'm trying
to hide it."

Q: What's the difference between a swan and
a lawyer?
A: One can stick its bill up its ass, the other
should.

Then there was the lawyer whose favorite
song was, *A Boy Named Sue* . . .

. . . the wit who pointed out that "criminal
lawyer" is redundant . . .

. . . and the bailiff who was known for putting on the writs.

The man accused of robbing a newsstand braced himself for cross-examination.

"Mr. Rufus," said the attorney, "considering what kind of a man you are, you have a fairly high degree of intelligence."

"Thanks," said Mr. Rufus. "If I weren't under oath, I'd return the compliment."

Another lawyer *wasn't* so sure about the intelligence of the robber he was representing. The man stole a half-million dollars from the bank, then had the nerve to go to the next teller and open a savings account. . . .

After being accused of assault and battery, Sonny said to the attorney, "I've got a half-million bucks. Can you get me off?"

"You have my word," said the attorney, "you will never go to jail with that much money."

The two muggers met in an alley, one of them breathless.

"I just tried to mug a lawyer," the man panted,

"Cripes," said the other. "He get anything?"

Then there was the British legal expert who was lecturing law students from the U.S. "Try not to confuse solicitors and barristers," he admonished them. "They're already confused enough."

It was obviously a losing cause, and defendant Curtis began to mutter bitterly to himself.

Scowling after several minutes of this, the judge said to Curtis's lawyer, "Mr. Moriarty, I'm calling a ten-minute recess. I want you to take your client outside and describe the kind of conduct that would be in his best interests."

The court recessed, and ten minutes later the lawyer entered alone.

"Where's your client?" asked the rather startled judge.

"The best advice I could give him was to split," said the attorney, "so he did."

Attorney Dickens bumped into one of his old law professors in Boston.

"How are you doing, Dickens?"

"Fine, sir. Since hanging out my shingle, I've acquired two clients."

"Just two?" said the professor. "They must be rich."

Dickens said, "They were."

"Why were you arrested?" the court-appointed attorney asked his client.

"For sneezing."

"How is that possible?" the lawyer asked.

"I sneezed in the museum and the night watchman woke up."

Then there was the judge who believed in wiping away a divorcee's tears with her ex-husband's bankbook . . .

. . . and the crooked judge who believed in dispensing with justice.

Judge Lutz was out campaigning in rural Virginia when his car broke down. Rather than go home, he borrowed a donkey, put a Vote for Lutz placard on its back, and continued going from door to door.

As he passed a farm, he waved. Looking up from his labors, one of the hands yelled, "Hey! Which of you is Lutz?"

The lawyer sat down with Mindy, a hooker who was arrested when a client was shot in her apartment.

"The police think you did it," said the attorney, "and the only way we can convince them otherwise is to present another suspect. Have you any idea who might have had it in for the dead man?"

"Search me," said Mindy.

"Business before pleasure," the lawyer replied.

⚖️

"Judge," said the innovative attorney, "you cannot send my client to jail. Admittedly, he cut a hole in the jewelry store window, reached in, and pulled out several rings and necklaces. But his brain was not in charge of his arm. It was acting of its own volition."

"I accept your argument," said the judge, "and I sentence your client's arm to ten years in prison. Whether he accompanies it or not is entirely up to him."

⚖️

"Your honor," said Ashton, "I would like to change my plea from not guilty to guilty."

"Why didn't you do this at the beginning of the trial and save us all the time and effort?"

"Because I thought I was innocent until I saw all the evidence you guys collected."

"Ten thousand dollars!" Mr. Marinelli shouted when the divorce lawyer quoted him a price. "Good lord, I can have her bumped off for *half* that!"

Then there was the prisoner who sent a card to his lawyer which read, "Serving a wonderful time. Wish you were here . . ."

. . . the brilliant Polish lawyer who could look at a contract and tell you immediately whether it was written or oral . . .

. . . and the South American natives who were brought to the big city to witness American justice. When they returned to their village, one of them said to the chief, "It is most amazing. One person says nothing, another person does all the talking, and twelve people listen. After they have listened, they judge the one who hasn't said a word!"

The founder of the law firm died, and all the partners and associates were there for the start of the funeral—except Jenson, who arrived a few minutes late.

"Have I missed anything?" he whispered to a colleague.

The lawyer said, "No. The rabbi's just opened for the defense."

Ostrovsky entered a crowded bar and sat at the counter. "Hey," he said to the bartender, "have you heard the joke about the two dumb lawyers?"

A man sitting next to Ostrovsky turned and tapped him on the shoulder. "Before you tell it," he said, "I want you to know that my friends and I are all lawyers."

"In that case," said Ostrovsky. "I'll tell the joke *real* slow."

When the defendant took the stand, the prosecutor rose, approached her, and said, "Ms. Flicker—in your own words, would you tell us what happened on the night of the murder?"

"If you don't mind," she said, "can I use my lawyer's words instead?"

Then there was the CEO of the large corporation who was on trial for embezzlement. However, his attorney mounted a clever defense.

"Why would my client embezzle money," said the attorney, "when there are so many legal ways to steal in this country?"

The CEO was acquitted.

Attorney Gittleson ran over to the office of his client Jake.

"I can't believe it! You sent a case of Dom Perignon to the judge? That guy's as straight as Abe Lincoln! Now we'll never win this case!"

"Relax," said Jake. "I sent it in the prosecutor's name."

A different defendant presented his lawyer with several bottles of champagne, after which the lawyer phoned and said, "There are only five bottles here. I can't make a case out of that."

When Mr. Mahoney sat down alone in the courtroom, the judge looked at him with surprise.

"You're charged with the serious crime of robbing five million dollars from an armored car. Why don't you have an attorney?"

"I did," Mahoney replied, "but when he found out I really didn't steal the money, he refused to represent me."

Xavier called an attorney from prison and said, "You've got to help me. I was arrested just because I'm a camera buff."

"Were you hauled in for taking pictures where you weren't supposed to?" asked the attorney.

"No. Cameras."

Then there was the divorce lawyer whose clients took each other for better or worse but not for good . . .

. . . and the other lawyer whose clients took each other for better or worse when they were married, then for everything when they divorced.

Disgusted that one juror was holding up a

guilty verdict in a mob trial, the judge dismissed him.

"You *can't* dismiss me!" the man insisted. Pointing to the defense attorney, he said, "*That's* the man paying my salary!"

Q: Why have many lawyers begun keeping skunks as pets?
A: Spare parts.

The attorney was reading the will to the members of the wealthy man's family. Reaching the end of the document, he said, "And to my wayward son Joseph, who I promised to remember in my will even though he has never worked a day in his life—hello there, Joseph!"

The district attorney was given the task of prosecuting the politician accused of forcing female employees to sleep with him.

"I hope you will find him guilty," the public defender said to the jury, "and return us to a time when politicians kissed babies *after* they were made. . . ."

⚖️

The lawyer ordered a new suit. When he went to pick it up, he was surprised to find something missing.

"Excuse me," he said to the tailor, "but where are the pockets?"

"Why do you need them?" the tailor asked. "What lawyer ever has his hands in his own pockets?"

⚖️

A late-night power outage killed the warning lights where Main Street intersected the train tracks, so old Mr. Sartwell was dispatched with his trusty flashlight to make sure there were no mishaps.

While he was on duty, there was a terrific accident as a car crossed the tracks at the same time as the 9:18 from New York came through. A trial ensued, during which Mr. Sartwell testified that he had waved his flashlight repeatedly at the car, but the car failed to respond.

The railroad was acquitted of negligence, after which the attorney took Sartwell aside.

"You did very well on the stand," she said. "Your testimony won the day."

"Aw, it wasn't me that won it," said Sartwell, "it was the other attorney."

"How so?"

"He should've asked if I remembered to turn the flashlight *on*."

It wasn't a good week for the railroad.

The trainload of thirty-six mules had crashed, killing all the animals. Everything was going well for the shipper in his suit against the railroad, until his attorney made his closing statement.

"Think of it," she said to the men and women, "thirty-six animals. Why, that's three times the number of jackasses there are on this jury!"

Then there was the lawyer who didn't bother to graduate from law school, but settled out of class . . .

. . . the attorney who wondered why Americans fight for freedom, then make laws to get rid of it . . .

. . . and the wag who defined America as a place whose citizens will try anything, except criminals.

"What makes you think your husband is unfaithful?" the divorce attorney asked his client.

"Well for one thing," she said, "he isn't even the father of my child!"

Hiram said to Myron, "I don't think my lawyer cares about my case . . . just about how much money he can wring from me."

"What makes you say that?"

"His bill," Hiram said. "Look at this: 'Twenty-five dollars for crossing the street to have a word with you, then discovering it wasn't you.'"

The priest settled into a chair in the lawyer's office.

"Is it true," said the priest, "that your firm does not charge members of the clergy?"

"I'm afraid you're misinformed," said the attorney. "People in your profession can look forward to a reward in the next world, but we lawyers have to take our reward in this one."

Young Tad was walking along the deserted lake when he heard a cry for help. Spotting a capsized boat in the water with a man flailing his arms nearby, he ran to the pier, threw another rowboat in the water, and rushed toward the helpless figure.

After pulling him in, Tad began rowing

back to shore. When the panting man could finally speak, he said, "Young fellow—I'm attorney Jerry Goldsmith, and I'm one of the richest men in town. For saving my life, I want to get you something . . . anything you want."

The boy thought for a moment, then said, "I'd like a nice funeral, if you please."

"A funeral?" gasped the lawyer. "You can't be more than twelve years old! Why are you thinking about dying?"

"Because when my dad finds out I saved a lawyer from drowning, he's gonna kill me."

The reporter from *The Law Gazette* asked the partner, "How many lawyers work in your office?"

"Oh," the partner replied, "about one in four."

Q: What's the difference between a tennis pro and a lawyer?
A: One stands in a court, the other lies.

Over lunch, attorney Nazarro said to a colleague, "I'm afraid I'm going to have to fire my secretary. She keeps coming in and asking me how to spell legal terms."

"Wow," said his friend, "that *can* be annoying."

"You're not kidding. I have to stop what I'm doing, get down the law book, look it up. . . ."

"Miss," said the attorney, "have you ever before been a witness in a suit like this?"

"No," said the woman. "Last time, I wore my white skirt and black blouse."

"I want a divorce," rich Melissa said to her attorney. "After a year, Richard managed to steal nearly a quarter-of-a-million dollars and then just drove off in one of my cars."

"The cad!"

"No, thank God, it was the Buick."

The judge asked the attorney from Ireland, "Do you care to challenge any of the jurors?"

The lawyer looked them over, then said, "I would. I think I can take that old gentleman in the back row."

Q: What's the difference between a lawyer and a caretaker at a petting zoo?

A: Nothing. Both work for does and bucks every hour.

The divorce lawyer asked Mr. Izzo, "Exactly what is it that keeps coming between you and your wife?"

Mr. Izzo replied, "The police."

As old attorney Nemeroff lay dying, he handed a Bible to his daughter, who was also an attorney.

"Would you like me to read to you, papa?"

Nemeroff shook his head weakly and said, "I want you to find the loopholes."

Taking the stand in the divorce hearing, Mrs. Kelly raged without provocation, "My husband is the slimiest, meanest, most underhanded—"

"You haven't been asked for your opinion," the judge interrupted.

"I know that, your honor, but I'm telling the truth!"

"I'm sorry," said the judge, "but we can't have any of that in here."

The lawyer asked the teenage boy, "What gear were you in at the time of the accident?"

"Let's see, man," said the youngster. "I had on hightops, shorts, and my shades."

Q: What's better than having the two best lawyers in the nation defend you?
A: Having one good witness.

Then there was the corrupt judge who was disappointed . . .

. . . and the lawyer who committed a civil wrong and was distorted.

Tilson was surprised when two men from the *Book of World Records* showed up at his front door early one morning.

"We're looking for Mr. Burt Tilson," said one. "At one hundred and twenty-eight, he's the oldest man alive."

"I'm Burt Tilson," he said.

The men looked at him with surprise.

"You can't be. You don't look like you're over fifty."

"I'm forty-seven," he said. "If you don't believe me, call my office. I'm an attorney with the firm of Grudge, Bose."

The men looked at each other. "Damn," said one. "Someone computed his age based on the number of hours he's billed."

Without looking up from his newspaper, the attorney said, "Can I have more coffee, please?"

His wife said, "Isn't it time you went to the office?"

The attorney looked up, startled. "You mean I'm *not* there?"

Henson went to see an attorney. "I need something to calm myself down."

"But I'm a lawyer, not a doctor."

"I know," said Henson. "What I need is a divorce."

"Why do you want to divorce your husband?" the attorney asked Mrs. Bridges.

"Before we have sexual relations, he always insists that I wash his chest with soap and hot water."

The attorney seemed surprised. "Surely you can understand how that might turn a man on."

"Oh, I do," she said. "But last night, when he came home late, his chest was clean."

The attorney, new in town, sat down at a testimonial dinner honoring the judge.

"Holy cow," said the attorney as he glanced up at the podium. "Do you mean to say that bald, bucktoothed, *ugly* man is Judge Woggins?"

A woman sitting beside him fired a withering look at the attorney.

"Do you know who I am?"

"No, ma'am."

"I'm *Mrs.* Woggins!"

"I see," said the lawyer. "Do you know who I am?"

"I certainly do not."

"Thank god," he said as he hurried away.

Then there was the divorce lawyer who described his job as helping women to get back their maiden aims. . . .

. . . the other divorce lawyer who was so articulate he was nicknamed, "The split lip . . ."

. . . and the woman who hired an attorney and charged her husband with reckless driving: she spotted him with another woman in the car.

Q: What do you call a lawyer who once played football for Philadelphia?
A: A legal Eagle.

The lawyer entered the prison cell and faced Abner. "Before you tell me anything about the crime, I'd like to know if there are any witnesses."

"There was only one other person in the room," he said. "My girlfriend, Olivia May."

"Great," said the lawyer. "I'm going to find her before the prosecutor does."

Two days later, the dejected attorney returned.

"No luck," he said to Abner. "I can't find a trace of Olivia May."

"I'm not surprised," said Abner. "She's the one I'm accused of having killed."

Then there was the attorney who pointed out that it only takes a few words in a church to get married, and a few words in your sleep to get divorced . . .

. . . and the lawyer whose book about his best closing arguments made the bestseller list under fiction. . . .

. . . and the lawyer who got his client acquitted because of conflicting testimony. The police claimed he shot the man in a bar, but the doctor said the victim was shot in the temple.

"Why do you want to be buried in the middle of the Atlantic Ocean?" the attorney asked Wenislaw as he drew up a new will.

"Because," said Wenislaw, "my wife has vowed to dance on my grave."

The bedraggled lawyer sat down at the bar and said to the bartender, "I'd like an Attorney Drink, please."

"How do you make an Attorney Drink?"

The lawyer said, "Take away his biggest client."

The divorce attorney arrived at the summer cottage of his client, Mr. Hausehalter. Much to his chagrin, Mrs. Hausehalter answered the door.

"Pardon me," he said, "but I need to speak with Mr. Hausehalter. Would you tell me where I can find him?"

"Certainly," the woman said graciously. "Just follow the river until you come to a fishing pole."

The attorney glanced behind him and saw several men fishing along the river's length. "How will I know which one is your husband?"

"That's simple. Just look for the pole with a worm on both ends."

The noted Republican fundraiser was on the stand.

"Mrs. Feinstein," said the lawyer, "you testified that my client mugged you in the mall, yet no one who was nearby heard your scream. Why is that?"

"Because," she huffed, "the Democratic candidate was speaking."

"So?"

"Well," she said, "I would have *died* if the Democrats thought I was cheering for them."

The elderly man attended the court proceedings for his brother, who was being tried for armed robbery. Throughout the hearing, a young boy sat beside him.

After a few days, the older man turned to the boy. "Young man, are you an habitué of hearings like these?"

"Yes, sir," the boy replied. "My dad's the prosecuting attorney."

"Ah," the man replied, "you're the son of a habitué."

Q: How does a convicted mob boss genuflect?
A: He gets down on his attorneys.

The woman stormed into the divorce lawyer's office. "I want a divorce from that philandering husband of mine!"

"Typical romantic triangle?" asked the lawyer.

"Triangle my ass," she said. "It's a goddam pentangle!"

While delivering his closing remarks in defense of the prostitute, the lawyer said, "You cannot single my client out. Although I have not gone to one of them, I know there are at least eight brothels in our fair city."

A voice cried from the back of the courtroom, "Which one?"

The attorney asked Mrs. de Sade, "Why did you decide to divorce your husband, the marquis?"

She replied, "Beats me."

"Mrs. Miller, you've been found guilty of stealing apples from your neighbor's orchard. What do you have to say for yourself?"

"It was a mistake, your honor."

"A mistake?"

"Yes, sir. I thought they were ripe."

Q: What's the difference between a member of congress and a lawyer?

A: One finds ways to pass laws, the other to bypass them.

The associate dragged himself into the law offices and complained to another associate, "I lost my last case."

The attorney said, "That would be nice."

Mrs. Franklin said to her attorney, "I'd like to divorce my husband."

"What are the grounds."

"He just doesn't go with the new furniture."

The woman said to her divorce attorney, "For twenty years, my husband and I were incredibly happy."

"Then what happened?" the attorney asked.

She replied, "We met."

After being found not guilty for stealing a diamond necklace, Dunbar went up to the judge.

"I want my attorney arrested!"

"Why?" the judge asked. "He got you acquitted!"

"I know," said Dunbar, "but I couldn't pay his fee so he took the damn necklace!"

The defendant said, "Your honor—I waive my hearing."

"What do you mean?"

"I mean," said the defendant, "I'm sick of this trial and I don't want to hear any more about it."

What is it called when . . .

  . . . St. Nick is sued? A Claus action suit.

  . . . decisions are handed down in June, July, and August? Summery judgment.

  . . . actress Shepherd is hauled before a judge? A Cybill suit.

. . . Gloria Steinem takes the stand? A ms. demeanor.

. . . someone testifies on behalf of the mayor of Palm Springs? Pro Bono.

. . . Keebler lands in court? Elf-incrimination.

. . . G. Gordon hires a lawyer? Liddygation.

. . . Ms. Brinkley is brought into a Texas court? Habeas Corpus Christie.

Mr. Wayne said to his attorney, "I want to divorce my wife. She hasn't spoken to me for weeks."

"I see," said the lawyer, "and you don't feel like you deserve such a good woman."

Q: A unicorn, an honest lawyer, and a little girl were walking down the street when they spotted a hundred dollar bill. Who got it?

A: The little girl; the other two are mythical beings.

Dora was on the stand, testifying about the murder of her boyfriend.

The prosecutor asked, "Before his death, you two were in Las Vegas, correct?"

"That's right."

"Would you mind telling us about the hotel incident?"

"Objection!" shouted her lawyer. "That was a year before the alleged crime."

"But I believe it has a direct bearing on the case," the prosecutor said.

Dora piped up, "It's all right, your honor. I'll answer."

"I wish you wouldn't," her lawyer said.

"Really, I don't mind."

"Very well," said the prosecutor. "Now—about the hotel incident?"

Fixing her big blue eyes on the prosecutor, Dora said, "As far as I know, there is no such place."

Then there was the judge who was offered a thousand dollar bribe from lawyer Smith, and a fifteen hundred dollar bribe from lawyer Jones.

Taking the lawyers aside, he handed five

hundred dollars to Jones and said, "Now I can decide the case on its merits alone."

Q: What's the difference between a fair trial and the evaporation of morning moisture?
A: Nothing. They're both due process.

"Did you hear about Chief Justice Piedmont?" one lawyer asked another.

"No! What happened?"

"He was out taking his morning stroll when a motorboat hit him."

"I'm in trouble and I need an attorney," said Belson as he sat down in the lawyer's office.

"Of course," said the attorney. "What are the charges?"

Belson seemed surprised. "Say—aren't I supposed to pay *you*?"

Boudoin was defending himself.

"Your honor, I think the officers were a bit hasty in their assessment of my condition. You see, I'd been drinking and I *was* intoxicated, but I wasn't inebriated."

"I accept your explanation," said the judge, "and instead of fining you a thousand dollars, I fine you a grand."

The lawyer broke the bad news to his client: the judge was sure to give him concurrent sentences for the multiple murders.

"What's wrong with that?" said the killer, who had expected to die.

"What's wrong," said the lawyer, "is that you're the con and the current is AC."

Then there was the woman who chaired the meeting of female attorneys. Complaining of disagreements over how to achieve economic parity with male attorneys, she said,

"As long as women are split as we are, men will remain on top. . . ."

~~⚖~~

Judge Infantino looked down at the unkempt man who was accused of robbing a fruit stand.

"Have you ever managed to earn a buck in your *life*?" the judge asked.

"Yes, sir. When I voted for you in the last election."

~~⚖~~

Actually, the judge who lost to Infantino knew about all of the votes his rival bought. Cornering a woman who'd been given a tendollar bill at the polling place, the judge said, "Miss—did you just vote for Infantino?"

"I don't see how it's any of your business," she said, "but—yes, I did."

"And might I ask why?"

"Sure. I like him."

The judge sneered. "I happen to know that one of his flunkies gave you ten dollars just to vote for him!"

"That's true," said the woman. "And when someone does that, you just *gotta* like him!"

"I know that thirty thousand dollars seems expensive," the attorney told a millionaire and prospective client, "but I throw myself completely into what I do."

The millionaire wrote out a check and handed it to the lawyer. "Please dig a very, very deep hole."

The judge said, "You're here for public lewdness, Mr. Moran. What do you have to say for yourself."

"I'm innocent, your honor."

"But didn't you expose yourself, and then urinate on a park bench?"

"I did," admitted Moran, "but I was only following instructions."

"Instructions? Whose?"

"Whoever left the sign that said, 'Wet Paint.' "

Show me . . .

. . . a Jewish kid who doesn't go to medical school and I'll show you a lawyer.

. . . an Italian judge who likes to eat and I'll show you a justice of the pizza.

. . . a kid who marries into a law firm and I'll show you an attorney-in-law.

. . . a lawyer who's gone on the wagon and I'll show you a lawyer who's been disbarred.

The lawyer and her husband were having a late dinner one night.

"I just don't understand," she said. "The law specifically states one thing, yet Judge Asherman made a point of disallowing—"

"Honey," said her husband, "for once—just *once*—why can't we talk about something other than the law or a case you're working on?"

"I'm sorry," she said. "What would you like to talk about?"

"How about sex?"

"Okay," she said. After a moment, she asked, "How often do you think Judge Asherman has sex?"

Then there was the divorce attorney who was fond of telling clients that marriage wasn't a word, it was a sentence . . .

. . . the lawyer who started out to do well, but only ended up well-to-do. . . .

. . . and the other divorce lawyer who told a colleague the surest sign that a man is in love is when he comes in to divorce his wife. . . .

Another divorce attorney was able to nail a wealthy husband who had run out on his new wife. Seems there was a clause in their prenuptial agreement that entitled her to a substantial penalty for early withdrawal. . . .

Accountant Kaplan met attorney Stiffson in the elevator.

"Nice weather we're having, huh?" Kaplan asked. As Stiffson was about to reply, Kaplan realized what he'd done and said, "Don't answer. I can't afford the fee for your opinion."

Priscilla sued her employer for wrongful dismissal, claiming he'd fired her because she refused to sleep with him.

Taking the stand, she was asked by her attorney to describe exactly what her boss had said.

Shifting uneasily, Priscilla said, "I—I can't. It's too vulgar."

"I see," said the attorney. "Your honor— could the plaintiff just write down what was said and pass it among the jury?"

"That will be fine," said the judge. "It will then be entered into the record."

Priscilla took pen in hand and wrote quickly, then handed the sheet of paper to the judge. He read it and then passed it to the jury.

When the note reached the eleventh juror, she was forced to elbow the juror next to her, who was sleeping. Awaking with a start, he took the note which read, *I want to screw you like no one has ever screwed you before.* Smiling, he put it in his pocket.

The judge looked at him. "Would juror number twelve mind reading the note for the record?"

"You're out of line, your honor," said the man. "It's just between me and the lady next to me."

One lawyer asked another, "How did Timothy feel when the judge ordered him to pay ten grand a month to his ex-wife?"

"Chagrined."

"What was her reaction?" the lawyer asked.

"She grinned."

Q: What's the difference between a defendant who's found innocent and one who's found guilty?

A: When the innocent one waves to the jury, he uses all five fingers.

Then there was the attorney who had case after case of hotdogs dropped on his lawn after he sued the French government and was awarded one million francs. . . .

Then there was the attorney who had case after case of hotdogs dropped on his lawn after he sued the French government and was awarded one million francs. . . .

The politician was standing trial for having committed adultery. He was acquitted because he had a clever lawyer who pointed out that politicians never commit themselves to anything. . . .

Angie said to her lawyer, "I want a divorce."

"Why?"

"Because I think my husband's cheating on me."

"Do you have any proof?" the lawyer asked.

"He *admitted* it!" she said. "Last night, we were sitting outside and he said, 'In the moonlight, your teeth are like pearls.' "

"What's wrong with that?"

"He wouldn't tell me who Pearl is."

Q: If a tall, skinny lawyer and a short, fat lawyer jumped off the Empire State Building, who'd land first?
A: Who cares?

Q: What did those two lawyers do as they plunged toward Thirty-Fourth Street?
A: Tried to find loopholes in the law of gravity.

Called into the judge's chambers, the attorneys immediately launched into a verbal volley.

"You are, without a doubt, the world's biggest fool!" said one.

"And you, my friend, are an insufferable ass!"

The judge shouted, "Counselors, have you forgotten that I am in the room?"

The attorney in South Africa raised eyebrows while arguing against the death penalty for his client, the wife of a political activist.

"It is my belief," said the lawyer, "that a woman should not be hung like a man. . . ."

The defense attorney rose and said, "Members of the jury—you've heard all the testimony, and now I want to tell you a few more things about my client.

"He's a good and kind man, a loving father and devoted husband. He visits his mother regularly, and is a regular churchgoer. At work, he's a model employee."

Listening to this, the defendant turned to his wife and said, "How do you like that? I give him a ton of money to defend me, and he goes and talks up some other guy!"

Q: What's the difference between a jury and a defendant in America?
A: At night, they lock up the jury and let the defendant go home.

Q: What's another difference between a jury and a defendant in America?
A: When a jury is hung, a killer can go free.

Small-town lawyer Lanny Rose had died without any survivors, so the townspeople took up a collection to bury him.

When they came to rich, old, cantankerous Mr. Tawney, they explained that they were burying attorney Rose and asked for a twenty-dollar donation.

The elderly man wrote out a check for a hundred dollars. "Here," he said. "Bury five of the bastards."

Coaching his client Ben before putting him on the stand, the attorney was concerned about the man's penchant for putting his foot in his mouth.

"Before you go up there," said the lawyer, "there are two things you must steadfastly avoid."

"What are those?"
The lawyer replied, "Nouns and verbs."

Then there was the lawyer who pointed out to his male client that "alimony" is actually a contraction for "all his money" . . .

. . . and the lady lawyer who discovered that it can take a little wile to win a case. . . .

. . . and the lawyer who instructed her daughter on the alleged facts of life.

Q: What did Henry VIII say to his solicitor?
A: "Alimony? Hell, I've got a better idea. . . ."

The attorney was addressing a group of high school kids during Career Week.

"Don't be afraid to dream," he said at the end of his speech. "When I was your age, and *Bonnie and Clyde* was the rage, I wanted to be a gangster like Clyde Barrow."

From the audience, one of the teenagers shouted, "How lucky you are to have realized your goal!"

The small-claims court judge scowled at Mr. Sousa. "Is it true that you stole this man's ladder?"

"Not really, your honor," said Sousa. "I only carried it to my house around the corner as a prank."

The judge was unmoved. "I fine you five thousand dollars. That was carrying a joke too far."

Mr. Cohan, the defendant, had struck a pedestrian with his car. At the trial, Mr. Cohan's attorney rose and said, "I ask the court to dismiss the charges. Look at my client's record: he's been driving for thirty years and has never even gotten a speeding ticket! The pedestrian was obviously in the wrong."

The plaintiff's attorney rose and said, "Following that train of thought, your honor, the charges cannot possibly be dropped. My client has never been hit by a car, and he's been walking for *sixty* years."

Then there was the pyromaniac who was found guilty and fired his lawyer . . .

. . . and the divorce attorney who refused to practice in Nevada. When asked why, he replied, "I haven't the Vegas idea."

The judge said to the two men, "This case is idiotic. Why couldn't you settle this out of court?"

"We tried to," said one, "but the cops came and broke it up."

Ninety-eight-year-old Mrs. Brisbee walked slowly into her attorney's office and sat down. "I want a divorce."

The lawyer looked at her with astonishment. "But Mrs. Brisbee—you and Mr. Brisbee have been married for seventy years! Why do you want a divorce *now*?"

The old woman said, "We wanted to wait till the children were dead."

After being found guilty, Burkow was wrapping things up with his lawyer.

"I'm sorry it turned out this way," said the lawyer.

"Me, too," said Burkow. "Especially since I was nowhere near the scene of the crime that night. I was in prison."

The attorney looked at him aghast. "You were in *prison*? Why didn't you *tell* me? That's an airtight alibi!"

Burkow said, "I was afraid it might prejudice the jury."

Rachel Hager had inherited a fortune, but the lawyer representing the estate was unable to find her. Consulting a private investigator, he explained the situation to the man.

"Don't worry," the detective said. "I'll find her."

A week later, the lawyer received a call.

"I've located Ms. Hager."

"Great! Where is she?"

"Here, with me," said the sleuth. "We were married this morning."

Q: What has eighteen legs and a hole in the middle?
A: The Supreme Court.

A lawyer and his two clients—a Jew and a Hindu—were driving through the countryside when their car broke down. Trekking to a nearby farm, they phoned a garage and were told the car couldn't be towed until morning.

The farmer said he'd be glad to put the men up, but he only had two beds: one of them would have to sleep in the barn.

The lawyer and Hindu took the bed and the Jew went to the barn. A few minutes later, the Jew knocked on the door.

"There's a pig in there, and my religion forbids me from sleeping with it."

The Hindu understood and agreed to take his place, but a few minutes later he knocked on the door.

"I'm sorry," he said, "but there's a cow in the barn and I am not permitted to lie with it."

Grumbling, the lawyer got up and went to sleep in the barn.

A few minutes later, the pig and cow knocked on the door. . . .

Then there was the brilliant attorney whose doctor told him he had only four weeks to live. The attorney managed to wrangle the first two weeks in January and the last two in December.

The attorney said to the witness, "Isn't it true, Mr. Pratt, that the only reason you're involved in this case is because you're an imbecile whom the prosecuting attorney has been able to manipulate?"

The man just stared into space without looking at the lawyer.

"I repeat," said the attorney. "Isn't it a fact that you are utterly and completely unqualified to be sitting up here?"

The man continued to stare. Finally, the judge said, "Mr. Pratt, would you please answer the question!"

"Me?" he said. "Good lord, I thought he was talking to you!"

Q: What's the difference between a lawyer and a prostitute?
A: Nothing. You pay them both to screw you.

Q: Actually, there is a difference between a lawyer and a prostitute. What is it?
A: There are some things even a hooker won't do for money.

The lawyer was hurrying home one night and ran a stop sign, smashing into a car driven by a little old man. Jumping from the car, the lawyer helped the old man from the wreck.

"You nearly killed me, sonny!" the elderly fellow was screaming. "Where the *hell* were you rushing?"

"I'm so sorry," said the attorney as he helped the man to the curb. "You look shaken—let me get you something."

Running back to his car, the lawyer made a call from his car phone, then opened the glove compartment and took out a flask. He brought it over to the old man.

"Here, have a sip of this."

Trembling, the old man took the flask and slugged down a shot.

"Feel better?"

"A little," said the old man.

"Have another. It'll calm you."

The old man did so, then had another. After his fourth drink, he looked crosseyed at the lawyer. "You ishn't havin' any?"

"No," said the lawyer. "I'm just going to sit here until the police arrive."

The counselor was interviewing Leslie, a prospective juror.

"I don't think I can serve," she said, "because I don't believe in the death penalty."

"That's all right," said the attorney, "this isn't a murder case. A man is being tried because his wife gave him the money she'd saved to buy plane tickets to Paris, and he lost the money at the track."

"I'll serve," said Leslie, "and forget what I said about the death penalty."

The baker burst into the lawyer's office. "Is the owner liable if his dog steals a loaf of bread?"

"He most certainly is," said the attorney.

"Then you owe me a dollar-fifty," said the baker. "Your dog snatched a loaf of bread."

"Fine," said the lawyer, and paid him. "Now you owe me fifty dollars for legal advice."

Q: How can you tell when lawyers are lying?
A: Their lips are moving.

The divorce attorney sat down with Mr. Main and spread out the pictures a private investigator had taken of Mrs. Main.

"This proves, beyond a doubt, that your wife has been having an affair," the lawyer said. "The case is open and shut."

Mr. Main shook his head. "I can't believe it. I just can't believe it."

"I'm afraid the affair is real—the photographs don't lie."

"No," said Mr. Main, "I mean, I can't believe that she's having so much fun!"

"Based on what you told me," the attorney said to Brown, "it's an open-and-shut case. The other guy hasn't got a leg to stand on."

"In that case," said Brown, "goodbye."

The lawyer was stunned. "Where are you going? I just gave you good news!"

"Sorry," said Brown, "but I told you *his* side of the story."

Then there was the judge who described verbal jousts between rival lawyers as attorneyment. . . .

. . . and the attorney who prided himself on being a wit in court. Actually, he was only half right. . . .

On the first day of the trial, the judge noted with alarm that there were only eleven jurors present.

"Who's missing?" he asked the foreman.

"Jimenez," said the woman. "He had to march in the Hispanic Day parade. But don't worry—he left his verdict with me."

The billionaire faxed his attorney: *How did the case turn out?*

The attorney faxed back: *Justice has triumphed!*

The billionaire faxed again: *Appeal at once!*

Q: What do you call a partner who hires new associates for the firm?
A: An emplawyer.

The newly arrived, small-town attorney watched as a man walked in the foyer. Knowing how important appearances are, the lawyer waited until the man was within earshot, then snapped up the phone.

"No," said the attorney, "I'm much too busy to take your case. I'm sorry—even for a ten-thousand-dollar retainer."

Hanging up, he turned to the man standing in his doorway. "What can I do for you?"

The man said, "I'm here to connect your phones."

The defendant sat in the courtroom as the charges against him were read.

"The City of New York vs. Colm Crawford."

Crawford leaned over to his attorney. "Imag-

144

ine that," he said. "Ten million people pissed at me because I ran a stop sign!"

Then there was the divorce attorney who said that while love is grand, divorce is many times that . . .

. . . and the attorney who was lost in thought. Seems it was unfamiliar territory.

Attorney Alexander was about to deliver his closing arguments in the terrorism trial of Hans Gruber.

While the lawyer began addressing the jury, Gruber turned to his co-counsel.

"What are my chances of escaping the chair?"

"Great," the lawyer said, "as long as Alexander keeps talking."

The attorney said to the defendant, "I just don't understand it. You robbed the convenience store because you said you were hungry. Why didn't you just steal the food instead of the money?"

The defendant said, "Because I've got my pride. I believe in paying for what I eat."

Billionaire Harvey Rochman said to his attorney, "I want it stipulated in my will that my wife inherits everything, but only if she remarries within six months."

"Why such an odd stipulation?"

Rochman replied, "I want *someone* to be sorry I died."

Davis was hauled into court in a trio of paternity suits.

"My client is innocent, your honor," said Davis's attorney, "by reason of insanity."

The judge looked at Davis, who was sitting serenely beside the lawyer.

"I don't know about that," said the judge. "He looks perfectly sane to me."

"Yes," said the lawyer, "but he's crazy about sex."

Q: What do a reformed drunk and JFK Jr. have in common?
A: Both had trouble passing the bar.

The Italian man was trembling as his lawyer showed up at the prison.

"Good news," said the attorney. "Even though you pushed your wife from a speeding car, then tried to run her over, I got you off."

"I want to stay here."

"But why?" the lawyer said. "She didn't die."

"I know," said the man. "That's why I want to stay here."

"My wife wants a divorce," Mr. Helms said to the attorney. "And after thirty-five years of marriage and twenty-nine kids, no less."

"You have twenty-nine children?" said the lawyer. "Forgive me for asking, but why didn't you go for a round thirty."

"Well that's just it," said Mr. Helms. "She wants to have a career, too."

⚖️

Then there was the brilliant attorney who managed to get his client's sodomy charge reduced to following too closely . . .

⚖️

. . . and the jurist who, as the trial entered its second month, complained to the judge that she was tired of being treated like a mushroom: kept in the dark and fed shit.

⚖️

The lawyer was a rabid Yankees fan, and he had a court date during the game that would decide the American League championship. Before leaving for court, he asked his wife to watch the game on TV.

When the judge called a five-minute recess, the lawyer bolted from the courtroom and shoved a quarter in the pay phone.

"What happened?" he asked.

"The game's over," said his wife. "The score was six to four."

"Who won?"

She replied, "The team with six."

Q: What do a weightlifter and a publicity-seeking lawyer have in common?

A: They're both well acquainted with the bench press.

The three children were caught stealing apples from farmer Bluejeans's orchard. The farmer brought them home to their parents and said he wouldn't press charges if the children were given a talking-to.

The next day, the children showed up at Bluejeans's door.

"My mom's a theology teacher," said one

boy, "and she said that God doesn't like stealers . . . so I'll never steal again."

"My dad's a doctor," said the next little boy, "and he said we could've got hurt climbing the tree and doing what we did . . . so I'll never steal again."

"My dad's a lawyer," said the third child, "and we're gonna sue you for the pants I tore on your tree."

The bratty kid didn't stop there, though. He hated one of his teachers and, having learned something of how the law works, presented one of Mr. Bluejeans's apples to his teacher. Later that day, he had him arrested for receiving stolen goods. . . .

Q: Why do lawyers fight so hard for free speech?
A: Because that's all their's is worth.

After sentencing the high-living mobster to ten years in prison, the judge ran to his chambers and pulled off his robes.

"What's wrong, your honor?" asked an aide. "Are you afraid the gang's going to come after you?"

"Hell no," the judge said as he bolted toward the door. "I want to rent his apartment."

Attorney Carlton was vacationing in Bermuda and met a beautiful young girl named Maria who worked at the hotel. The two made love, and Carlton vowed that he'd return to her the following year.

True to his word, he flew back to the island, checked into the hotel, and was surprised to find that Maria had a three-month-old baby.

"It's yours," she said sweetly.

Carlton was astonished. "Why didn't you tell me? I love you, Maria. I'd have been proud to marry you."

She said, "I talked it over with my parents, but we decided we'd rather have a bastard in our family than a lawyer."

During his opening statement, attorney Hecht was startled when opposing attorney Hill leapt to his feet and shouted, "Hecht! You're an unctuous, prevaricating shyster!"

Flushing, Hecht shot back, "And you, Hill, are a mindless, talentless, arrogant bag of wind!"

"Why you *asshole*—!"

"Thimblewit!"

Banging his gavel, the judge said, "Now that you gentlemen have introduced one another to the court, may we proceed with the case?"

Q: How was the undertaker able to bury the attorney in a shoebox?

A: Instead of embalming him, he gave him an enema.

After reviewing his client's dossier, the attorney said, "When we go in to court tomorrow, I want you to plead insanity."

"But why? I'm not insane!"

"I know," said the lawyer, "but you'll find it easier breaking out of the loony bin than out of the stir."

The lawyer sat down with the family of the deceased millionaire and read his will.

"Being of sound mind and healthy body, I spent everything before I croaked. . . ."

The prosecutor said to the thief, "So you're admitting that you broke into Mr. Renkin's store and stole twenty TV sets, fifteen VCRs, and ten laserdisc players."

"I am," said the defendant, "but I deserve clemency. The loss wasn't as big as it could have been."

"Not as big?" said the attorney. "That's his entire stock!"

"True," said the crook, "but they were on sale."

Trying to score points with the Italian jury, the attorney said, "Show me a Protestant, and I'll show you a complete bunghole."

The judge said sternly, "I'm Protestant."

Without missing a beat, the attorney said, "Then take a look. I'm a complete bunghole."

Q: What did the lawyer do after losing a case for the Mafia?

A: He got blasted.

The lawyer cornered the doctor at a party and said, "In your opinion, which side is best to lie on?"

The doctor replied, "The side that has the most money."

The prosecutor was questioning the burly defendant.

"Exactly how hard did you punch the plaintiff?"

"Not hard."

"He says you broke his jaw."

"That's baloney."

"Would you mind *showing* the court what you did?"

"Whaddya mean?"

The prosecutor tapped his outthrust chin. "Hit me so the jury can see how hard you hit the plaintiff."

The defendant looked at the judge, who nodded. Exhaling, he rose, walked over to the prosecutor, and hit him so hard the man flew off his feet, tumbled over the front row of the jury, and landed in a heap in the back row.

The defendant said, "I hit him about one-eighth that hard."

After working late one night, the lawyer and his client went out for dinner. As they were walking down the deserted street, two men came up to them with pistols.

"Let's have your money," said one of the thugs.

Without hesitation, the client reached into his pocket, withdrew a wad of bills, and shoved it into the lawyer's hands.

"Why are you giving that to me?" the lawyer asked.

The client replied, "That's what I owe you for tonight's consultation."

The judge studied the man standing before him. "Have you ever been before me?"

"No I haven't, your honor."

"Ever been a witness?"

"No, your honor."

"That's very strange," the attorney said. "Your face looks familiar."

"Yes, your honor. I tend bar across the street."

Another judge studied the man standing before him. "Have you ever been before me?"

"No, your honor."

"Are you sure?"

"Yes, your honor."

"Then how do I know you?"

The man said, "I gave your daughter singing lessons."

The judge said, "Twenty years."

Q: What do you call it when a feminist takes
   the stand
A: Trial and ERA.

Then there was the preacher who was delivering a sermon and made a mistake, refer-
ring to the devil as the father of all lawyers
instead of the father of all liars. But the error
was so insignificant that he didn't bother to
correct himself.

Morrow was on trial for killing his wife.
Taking one look at the all-female jury, he
knew he was headed for the electric chair.

Managing to slip a note and five thousand
dollars to one of the jurors, he said, "This is
yours, with another five grand to follow if you
get me out of this with manslaughter."

The trial took its course and, when the jury
foreman read the verdict, manslaughter it
was. Morrow cheered as the judge sentenced
him to fifty years in prison.

As Morrow was led away, he passed by the juror. "I can't thank you enough," he said. "How'd you manage to do it?"

"It wasn't easy," the woman admitted. "The other eleven wanted to acquit you."

After empaneling a jury consisting largely of men, the lawyer said to his young client, Monica, "When the trial begins, I want you to wear hot pants and a halter top."

"But it's the middle of the winter!"

"Look," said the attorney, "do you want to be warm or acquitted?"

In the midst of his closing argument, the lawyer said, "If the truth be told, I'm a man of few words."

"That may be," someone in the courtroom said, "but you're keepin' 'em all mighty busy!"

The partners were deciding whether or not to take on a new client.

"Can he pay his bills?" said one.

"He's worth in the neighborhood of a half-billion dollars," said the other.

"Then let's take him on," said the other. "I've always liked that neighborhood."

Author David Peter was testifying in a case of copyright infringement.

"I am the greatest living writer," said the scribe.

"What gives you the right to say that?" asked the attorney.

"I've no choice," said Peter. "I'm under oath."

Gibbs was arrested for panhandling, and sat in the courtroom beside three gaudily dressed women.

"What is your profession?" the judge asked the first woman.

She stopped chewing her gum long enough to say, "I'm a model."

"My foot you are!" said the judge, and gave

her a thirty-day sentence. He looked at the next woman. "What is your profession?"

"I'm a street mime," she said.

"In a pig's eye!" snapped the judge, and sentenced her to thirty days. He faced the third woman. "What is your profession?"

"I'm a hooker," she said.

The judge smiled. "Young lady, I disapprove of your profession, but I appreciate your candor. I sentence you to thirty days, suspended." He looked at Gibbs. "And what is your profession, young man?"

"To tell you the truth," said Gibbs, "I'm a hooker, too."

The judge said to Cannell, "This is the fourth time you've been before me this month. What do you have to say for yourself?"

"Your honor," said Cannell, "when I like someone, I give him *all* my business."

The next time Cannell came into court, the judge said, "Last time I fined you fifty dollars—this time, it's one hundred."

"Hey," said Cannell, "don't I get a bulk discount?"

The judge said to the defendant, "You've been found guilty and are ordered to pay damages of ten thousand dollars. However, since you've been so contemptuous of this court during the proceedings, I assess you another hundred dollars. How does that strike you?"

The defendant smiled. "Extra fine."

Q: What's the difference between one lawyer in a small town and two lawyers in a small town.

A: One can earn an okay living, but two can make a fortune.

Varley said to his friends in the steam room, "I don't know why you're all trashing lawyers. Why, a lawyer once made me an outright gift of one thousand dollars."

"Is that a fact?" said one friend.

"It is. She won me forty thousand dollars in a malpractice settlement. Her bill was forty-one thousand dollars, and she let the extra grand slide."

What . . .

- . . . kind of songs do attorneys sing? Lawyairs.
- . . . can be found under attorneys' hats? Lawyhairs.
- . . . do attorneys hear with? Lawyears.
- . . . propels canoes filled with attorneys? Lawyoars.
- . . . sort of mistakes do attorneys make? Lawyerrs.
- . . . is the best place for attorneys to grow grass? Lawyards.
- . . . famous attorney once played hockey? Lawyorr.

As the judge was stepping up to the bench, he tripped and fell. The court clerk ran over to help him.

"I hope your Honor is all right," said the clerk.

"My honor is fine," said the judge. "It's my ass that hurts."

Then there was the lawyer who pointed out that the United States is a country where the lawns are well-kept and the laws aren't. . . .

. . . and the judge who admonished a witness, "If you get any further from the truth, you're going to be out of the jurisdiction of this court."

The attorney stood before St. Peter.

"What have you done to earn a place in Heaven?"

"Well, I was able to get a conviction against one of the most notorious mobsters in the world."

St. Peter looked down at his Book of Deeds. "I see no record of that. When was it?"

The lawyer said, "About three minutes ago."

Q: Where did the mountaineer go to sue the
   manufacturer of his faulty equipment?
A: Small-climbs court.

A Short Knock-Knock Story

Knock, knock.
Who's there?
Amana.
Amana who?
Amana need a lawyer.

Knock, knock.
Who's there?
Amahl.
Amahl who?
Amahl lawyer.

Knock, knock.
Who's there?
Watkin
Watkin who?
Watkin I do for you?

Knock, knock.
Who's there?
Willy.
Willy who?
Willy went to City Hall.

Knock, knock.
Who's there?
Demerit.
Demerit who?
Demerit me when he found me there!

Knock, knock.
Who's there?
Eiffel.
Eiffel who?
Eiffel down a flight of stairs!

Knock, knock.
Who's there?
Brokaw.
Brokaw who?
Brokaw my arm and two ribs.

Knock, knock.
Who's there?
Lasso.
Lasso who?
Lasso the city for a million bucks!

Knock, knock.
Who's there?
Gotti.
Gotti who?
Gotti little problem, though.

Knock, knock.
Who's there?
Iowa's.
Iowa's who?
Iowa's there to rob the place.

Knock, knock.
Who's there?
Snow.
Snow who?
Snow problem! You'll make *more* money suing them!

Knock, knock.
Who's there?
Isle.
Isle who?
Isle love the justice system!

A Shorter Knock-Knock Story

Knock, knock.
Who's there?
Idi.
Idi who?
Idi you pay your creditors, or you go to jail!

Knock, knock.
Who's there?
Amin.
Amin who?
Amin bankruptcy, but I've got to pay my lawyer.

Knock, knock.
Who's there?
Entebbe.
Entebbe who?
Entebbe represented in court, you've got to pay the lawyer up front.

Knock, knock.
Who's there?
Uganda.
Uganda who?
Uganda scape the long arm of the lawyer!

LAUGH 'TIL YOU CRY!

☐ **REFRIED NEWS by James Curley.** Read all about it—the world is whackier than ever! Here's all the news that's fit to make you howl!
(171322—$4.99)

☐ **THE OFFICIAL HANDBOOK OF PRACTICAL JOKES by Peter van der Linden.** A treasury of 144 rib-tickling tricks and leg-pulling pranks. This book will make your eyes water with laughter at the weirdest, wildest, most outrageously inventive and ingenious practical jokes ever assembled.
(158733—$3.50)

☐ **THE SECOND OFFICIAL HANDBOOK OF PRACTICAL JOKES by Peter van der Linden.** A good offense is the best defense, and with this book in your hands you'll have some of the zaniest, funniest, most inventive practical jokes ever assembled.
(169247—$3.50)

☐ **500 GREAT IRISH JOKES by Jay Allen.** Who are the nattiest men in Ireland? Find out the answer to this (and 499 more hilarious jokes)!
(168968—$3.50)

☐ **500 GREAT JEWISH JOKES by Jay Allen.** Why did the Jewish mother have her ashes scattered in Bloomingdale's? Find out the hilarious answers to this one—and many more!
(165853—$3.50)

Prices slightly higher in Canada

Buy them at your local bookstore or use this convenient coupon for ordering.

NEW AMERICAN LIBRARY
P.O. Box 999, Bergenfield, New Jersey 07621

Please send me the books I have checked above.
I am enclosing $_____ (please add $2.00 to cover postage and handling).
Send check or money order (no cash or C.O.D.'s) or charge by Mastercard or VISA (with a $15.00 minimum). Prices and numbers are subject to change without notice.

Card #_____ Exp. Date _____
Signature_____
Name_____
Address_____
City _____ State _____ Zip Code _____

For faster service when ordering by credit card call **1-800-253-6476**

Allow a minimum of 4-6 weeks for delivery. This offer is subject to change without notice.